This book should be returned to any branch of the Lancashire County Library on or before the date shown

FOR THE LOVE OF

RUNNING

FOR THE LOVE OF RUNNING

First published as *The Joy of Running* in 2013

Summersdale Publishers Ltd
46 West Street
Chichester
West Sussex
PO19 1RP
UK

www.summersdale.com

Printed and bound in the Czec

ISBN: 978-1-78685-015-7

Substantial discounts on bulk quantities of Summersdale books are available to corporations, professional associations and other organisations. For details contact general enquiries: telephone: +44 (0) 1243 771107, fax: +44 (0) 1243 786300 or email: enquiries@summersdale.com.

FOR THE LOVE OF
RUNNING

A COMPANION

PAUL OWEN

summersdale

To Fiona, Megan and James.
Thank you for explaining apostrophes.
My head hurts. I'm going for a run.

CONTENTS

INTRODUCTION

You never forget your first time do you? Mine was a hot, sweaty affair at the seaside which lasted just over four hours and fourteen minutes that left me dehydrated, exhausted and totally smitten. Blackpool Marathon took place in the middle of a heatwave at the height of summer on 19 June 2005, and I spent six months training, thinking about and preparing for the race. I still recall the feelings I had at the time, of excitement, anticipation, self-doubt and ultimately relief once I reached the finish line... oh, and the soreness that meant I could hardly walk for days. As soon as I could, the desire to repeat my brief encounter started leading to regular trips to the post box with race-entry forms. Despite many subsequent wonderful running experiences, Blackpool will always stay with me as the place that I lost my marathon virginity.

The act of running has played a pivotal role in the evolution of humanity since the birth of mankind. It has been important to many different civilisations throughout the ages for a wide variety of reasons. Early hunters relied on foot power to support their carnivorous diet; armies deployed long-distance runners to relay messages; the ancient Olympics was initially a religious festival combining ceremony and athletic endeavour; promoters staged races and charged the public to watch, and running was central to the development of a wide variety of sports such as rugby and football. Running races of one form or other have been popular for thousands of years, and to this day continue to attract both professional and amateur athletes the world over. The growth of participants in organised races continues to spiral upwards, with today's runner being able to choose from pure athletic races, obstacle-based events or those that involve another sport, such as triathlons. We have the luxury of being able to pick and choose what we enter, where we go and how we get there. The internet and budget airlines have contributed to the rise in the number of 'running tourists', who think nothing of hopping on a flight to another country just to enter a race, before returning to work the next day with their colleagues none the wiser. Closer to home, the parkrun phenomenon has brought fun, free and pressure-less access to 5 k events up and down Britain.

The benefits of being a runner are vast. Not only can it aid weight loss and alleviate the symptoms of depression, assist with sleeping problems and extend life expectancy, it can also help us to escape momentarily from the pressures of life. It can lead to friendship, love and an improved sex life. Far from causing problems such as 'runner's knee', it can actually help prevent injury as bone density increases even in older athletes. It can take you to places that you might never have gone, and to see things that you might never have seen. For me, that has meant watching the sun rise and fall from the side of mountains, experiencing the beauty of a trail run in every weather condition, discovering the stillness and peace of running throughout the night and early morning, marvelling in the wonder of nature in all its glory and, perhaps most importantly, reawakening a level of enjoyment for the sport that had been locked away for too many years; an enjoyment that can be shared with anyone who laces up a pair of running shoes and simply runs, no matter the distance, speed or terrain. I hope I can share that enjoyment with you.

Note on timings: All race times are given in the following format:

Hours: minutes: seconds. milliseconds

For example, 38 minutes, 50 seconds and 3 milliseconds appears as 38:50.3, and 38 hours and 50 seconds appears as 38:00:50.

A BRIEF HISTORY OF RUNNING

• •

" Every morning in Africa, a gazelle wakes up. It knows it must run faster than the fastest lion or it will be killed. Every morning a lion wakes up. It knows it must outrun the slowest gazelle or it will starve to death. It doesn't matter if you are a lion or a gazelle: when the sun comes up, you'd better be running. "

DAN MONTANO

RUNNERS THAT TIME FORGOT

Whilst Palaeolithic cave paintings don't depict early *Homo erectus* wearing the now-famous striped footwear of Mr Adi Dassler, or the 'swoosh' design of a certain American sports brand, science  can tell that humans developed the ability to run primarily to survive. Before the invention of 24-hour convenience stores, foot power was the main way to catch prey or scavenge carcasses before other predators arrived on the scene. Science can't say for certain why pre-humans became bipedal, and if the ability to run was a by-product of being able to walk upright on two limbs or the central factor in the evolution of the human body as it is now. Nevertheless, once upright, *Homo erectus*, *neanderthalensis* and subsequently *sapiens* all used one of their greatest strengths to maintain a carnivorous protein-rich diet. Whilst never the fastest movers, they were capable in terms of endurance of eventually outrunning any animal on Earth over a long distance, which remains the case to this day.

Depending upon which evolutionary camp your modern, well-cushioned foot is in, arguably humans' ability to run has led to every single advance and development in history. Running has been central to each civilisation that has ever existed, for a wide variety of survival, social and economic reasons.

IT'S A QUESTION OF SPORT

There is little historical evidence identifying when running for sport first occurred. Races certainly took place in ancient Egypt even before the great pyramids were built, and monuments to the pharaohs circa 2000 BC show that various sports were up and running, including athletics. Evidence of organised running has been found at Memphis, Egypt, dating back to circa 3800 BC. Pottery from ancient Greece also shows that running was used for both political and social reasons, as it depicts warriors sprinting into battle and shieldless men running for pleasure.

By the birth of the ancient Olympic Games in Olympia in 776 BC, the use of running as a spectacle had been established. The first Olympics was linked to religious festivals in honour of Zeus, King of the Gods, although races were not part of a particular ceremony. Initially there was only one short stadion race likely to have been around 200 yards long, which was won by a cook from Elis called Koroibos. A second, longer event was introduced 13 festivals later in 724 BC, when four more race distances were eventually added to the schedule. The final one, called a *hoplitodromos*, was added to the sixty-fifth Olympiad in 520 BC, which required competitors to carry a shield and armour. King Tahaka instituted a 100 km race for his soldiers between 690 and 665 BC, which has been recreated in the 100 km Pharaonic Race. Hieroglyphics from the time suggest the King himself took part.

The early races allowed only male entrants, and they were watched by men, boys, unmarried women and the priestess of Demeter, the goddess of fertility, who sat in a position of privilege on a marble throne, next to the altar in the stadium itself. Married women were prohibited from attending on penalty of death.

Unmarried women had their own festival dating back to the sixth century BC, called Heraia. Occurring every four years at Olympia, it was held in honour of the wife of Zeus, Hera. The only event was a footrace on a shortened track for three separate age groups. Unlike their nude male counterparts, women were allowed to wear knee-length tunics. The events open to women remained limited for a long period, but there is evidence indicating that the festival eventually expanded to include chariot races, nude wrestling and the javelin. Girls were not encouraged to be athletes unless they were from Sparta. The Spartans believed that healthy women produced healthy members of society, and so trained men and women in the same events.

For many years, the Spartans' view was not shared by the wider Greek society, and men and women did not compete at the same festivals until after the Greek Classical period. There are limited historical references as to when they began competing regularly at the same Games. One inscription dating back to first century AD records the names of young women who competed in footraces in Delphi, Isthmia and Nemea, but it is likely that the events at this time were still women-only affairs. Vases found at Arkteia from the fifth century AD depict women in short chitons in what appears to be a running contest.

One of the greatest battles in history took place at Marathon in 490 BC. The Persian King Darius I's army landed seeking to conquer Greece and came toe to toe with the Athenians as they did so. During this period, *hemerodromes* (day runners) were used widely to courier messages very long distances. Before the battle, a professional Greek messenger by the name Pheidippides is said to have run over 150 miles in 48 hours to seek help from Sparta for the Athenians, a feat which would go on to inspire the Spartathlon Ultra Race.

After the battle, Pheidippides supposedly ran a further 26 miles to carry news of the victory to Athens, uttering on arrival, 'Joy to you, we've won', before promptly keeling over and dying from exhaustion. His exploits and death were recorded and passed down through the ages in various literary forms including a poem by Robert Browning. It is this poem that is believed to be the inspiration for Baron Pierre de Coubertin and fellow founders of the modern Olympic Games to invent a race celebrating the achievements of the 40-year-old messenger, which they called the Marathon. By choosing the 26-mile distance, the Baron and his chums also inadvertently introduced 'the wall', which every marathoner will know can happen at around the 18- to 20-mile point, as the body's energy sources start to run out of fuel. 'Why couldn't Pheidippides have died here?' an athlete named Frank Shorter is attributed to have said to fellow runner Kenny Moore at the 16-mile point of one of his earliest marathons.

As race clocks and timing systems hadn't been invented, the precise times of the first Olympians are not known, although the results are. Léonidas of Rhodes was the Usain Bolt of his day, winning three races in the 164 BC Games and repeating the feat in the three Games that followed. Both Léonidas and Bolt have been declared the greatest sprinters of all time and reaped the rewards. Léonidas picked up an olive branch and the adulation of the country. Bolt had picked up $32.5 million by 2016, made thirty-second place on Forbes' The World's Highest-Paid Athletes list and has the adulation of pretty much every athletics fan on the planet.

The ancient Olympics continued after the Romans invaded Greece during the First Mithridatic War (89–85 BC) until AD 393, when the Christian Emperor Theodosius I shut off the oil lamps, believing the Games to be a pagan festival. By this time, it was 1,169 years after Elis had become the first Olympic running champion. Charismatic French nobleman, Baron Pierre de Coubertin, would be the driving force behind the Games' reappearance, but until then, the athletics world would have to wait another 1,506 years.

A DOMESTIC AFFAIR

There is little evidence to document when domestic races first began to appear around the world. However, a number of those that were successful are still running to this day. In Italy, the Palio del Drappo Verde of Verona lays claim to being one of the oldest footraces – an assertion supported by the Association of Road Racing Statisticians. Approximately 7–8 km in length, it reportedly dates back to 1208 and was held for 590 years before an enforced break during the French Revolutionary War in 1798, when the Papal States were invaded by France. It was restored as a 10 k race in 2008, and expanded into a non-competitive race of 9 km and a competitive race over 21.1 km by 2016.

In Britain, a fell race took place in Braemar, Scotland, circa 1040, believed to have been set up by King Malcolm with the aim of finding a modern day *hemerodrome*. Similar events appeared sporadically in the years that followed, but it was not until the mid-nineteenth century that fell races became regular events in the Scottish highlands. The modern Braemar Gathering, which has been running since 1832, now attracts international athletes, and the programme of events includes a relay, a sprint and a hill race.

The Red Hose Run 3 k was first held in Carnwath, Scotland, in 1508 under a royal charter issued by King James IV to John, third Lord Somerville:

" Paying thence yearly... one pair of hose containing half an all of English cloth at the feast of St John the Baptist, called Midsummer, upon the ground of the said barony, to the man running most quickly from the east end of the town of Carnwath to the Cross called Cawlo Cross. "

Hose is a Scots term for stockings or long socks, and the first female winner to 'sock it' to the men was Skye Dick in 2012, by which time the race had expanded to 4.5 km. For her efforts, Skye won – yes, you guessed it – a pair of socks. The race has been absorbed into the local agricultural show and it has been staged over 500 times.

I'LL HAVE A GUINEA ON MY MAN

By the sixteenth century, cross-country running was a part of English public school life, with its emphasis on outdoor activity being good for the mind and the body. Events such as Paper Chase (or Hare and Hounds) involved a lead runner known as the 'hare' laying a trail of paper for the 'hounds' to follow and would eventually lead to the formation of gentlemen's running clubs incorporating 'hare and hounds', or 'harriers', in their names. These schools could only be accessed by the wealthy, and the instilling of athletics into impressionable young minds partly explains the popularity of the rich placing large wagers on their man servants in specifically designed events of huge distances. Excessive gambling occurred in a wide variety of sports and athletics did not go untouched, despite the attempts of the authorities through laws such as the Gaming Act 1664.

Over the course of the next few centuries, professional runners would become commonplace. One of the first was the much celebrated Foster Powell (1734–1793), who was dubbed the 'Astonishing Pedestrian'. Powell's feats of endurance included walking and running from London to York and back again in six days for a 100-guinea wager in 1773, which he beat in 1787 aged 58, taking five days, 15 hours and 15 minutes. He was able to keep up a pace and cover distance that many current recreational runners would not be able to match despite wicking clothes, minimalist footwear and space-age technology. If required, he could run fast but his forte and livelihood were best served in huge mile-gobbling events.

PROFESSIONAL RUNNERS

Hot on the non-blistering heels of Powell were a succession of long-distance walkers and runners who increasingly pushed the boundaries of what was deemed possible by foot power alone. John Bryant recounts the case of Captain Robert Barclay Allardice in *The London Marathon,* who, for a 1,000-guinea wager in 1809, covered 1,000 miles in 1,000 consecutive hours at no more than one mile per hour. A runner named Moorex, 'the Italian giant', then repeated the feat in 1862 from Warren house, Lindley Moor in West Yorkshire. Bryant and London Marathon director Dave Bedford thought it would be fun to recreate the attempt over the seven weeks before the 2003 race. The competitors were almost all experienced long-distance athletes: Rory Coleman,

Shona Crombie-Hicks, David Lake, Paul Selby, Sharon Gayter and Lloyd Scott. To add a little extra to the challenge – as if that were needed – the final mile coincided with the start of the London marathon and each competitor had to finish that as well. Five of the six finished the challenge, with Scott having withdrawn after 355 miles. Each competitor received £6 for every mile they completed, £1,000 for completing the challenge, an additional £1,000 for finishing the marathon in under seven hours and £3,000 to the first male and female home in the race. Crombie-Hicks crossed the line in 3:08, Gayter in 3:34, Selby 3:44, followed by Lake, who finished his first marathon in 4:15, and Coleman in 4:21.

By the 1870s, six-day races on indoor tracks with substantial prize money on offer were quite commonplace. In 1878, a series of five international six-day events was created called the Astley Belt for the 'Long Distance Challenge Championship of the World', which was open to walkers and runners alike. This came about as a result of 70,000 people coming to watch an earlier two-man race featuring American Edward Payson Weston and Irish Daniel O'Leary, both of whom earned extraordinary money due to their athletic prowess. O'Leary claimed a world record best in an astonishing distance of 520.25 miles. The following year, in another event, Charles Rowell of Great Britain won $20,398 in one race: around 40 times more than the average working man's salary. In 1882 in Madison Square Gardens George Hazael became the first man to run 600 miles in six days.

The long-distance events were not exclusively male, with women such as Mary Marshall of Chicago, Amy Howard of

New York and British athlete Ada Anderson competing in the six-day events which were designed to maximise the profit from the beguiled public. They were also not limited to Britain and the States; in 1882, William Edwards emerged the winner in a six-day event in Australia, covering 432 miles in the process.

AMATEUR ATHLETIC ASSOCIATION (AAA)

In response to the growing number of professional races, the AAA was inaugurated in the Randolph Hotel, Oxford, in 1880 to protect the amateur principles of clubs, including the University's athletic club, Mincing Lane Athletic Club (formed in 1863 and now known as the London Athletic Club), Thames Hare & Hounds (formed in 1868) and clubs that followed such as Ranelagh Harriers (formed in 1881). The AAA promoted the purity of running for the act itself rather than for any form of financial gain. This ethos brought it into direct opposition with promoters who created large-scale events with prize money, aimed at the public's desire for a flutter. The conflict between professional runners and their gentleman counterparts remained well after the formation of the AAA.

The wealthier amateurs may not have needed the prize money to buy the Xbox equivalent of the day, but runners such as builder Len Hurst did. He won the first professionally staged 40 km marathon in 1896 between Paris and Conflans in 2:31:30. Just two months after the first time the race had been run in the modern Olympics, Len beat Spyridon Louis' record of 2:58:50.

It's not known if his speed was developed as a result of a long history of escaping disgruntled clients.

The professionals ran for prize money and tended to train harder than amateurs, for whom it was important to be seen to be winning without trying. This attitude is perfectly captured in the fact-based film *Chariots of Fire*. Harold Abrahams was an amateur who tried to break the mould. He used a professional coach, Sam Mussabini, to help him win the 1924 Olympic 100 m – a tactic that, for amateurs, was years ahead of its time. It is now standard amongst professional athletes on all continents and yet, back then, it flew in the face of the amateur ethos, and arguably held the sport back for much of the first half of the twentieth century. Fortunately for modern runners, Abrahams' views prevailed, and through lifelong commitment to the sport, he changed the face of British athletics and its laws forever, eventually ascending to the giddy heights of chairmanship of the AAA.

FASCINATING FACT

Bedford-born Harold wasn't the first athlete in the family. His brother Sidney 'Solly' Abrahams competed in the 1906 Intercalated Games and came eleventh in the long jump at the 1912 Games. Harold dined with New Zealander Arthur Porritt, who won Bronze in the 1924 final, every year on the anniversary of the race until the former's death in 1978.

The need for a worldwide governing body codifying different countries' rules and regulations was self-evident as international athletic competitions grew larger and more popular. The conflict between different codes was seen in the controversial men's 400 m final at the 1908 Olympic Games in London. British athlete Wyndham Halswelle had reached the final with a new record time of 48.4 seconds when he met three Americans, including John C. Carpenter. In the race, Carpenter ran diagonally and blocked Halswelle with his elbows, forcing the Scot to the side of the track – a tactic which was allowed in the US but not in the UK. Race official Roscoe Badger called a foul and the race was ordered to be re-run without Carpenter. His fellow countrymen in the race, William Robbins and John Taylor, declined to run meaning that Halswelle ran on his own. He claimed the easiest gold medal in the Games' entire history. It was events such as this that led 17 national athletics federations to establish the International Amateur Athletics Federation (IAAF) just four years later, on 17 July 1912. The IAAF remained resolutely amateur for 60 years before moving into the professional arena in 1982, followed in 1985 with the establishment of trust funds for athletes.

> ❝ *Play not only keeps us young but also maintains our perspective about the relative seriousness of things. Running is play, for even if we try hard to do well at it, it is a relief from everyday cares.* ❞
>
> **JIM FIXX, *THE COMPLETE BOOK OF RUNNING***

ACROSS THE POND

The first official amateur race in the history of the United States of America took place in November 1896, just months ahead of one of the most famous marathons in the world: the Boston Marathon. It was the eight-kilometre YMCA Turkey Trot in Buffalo, New York, and saw just six runners compete along a five-mile course, won by Henry A. Allison. Fast forward to 2016 and the race now regularly tops 14,000 entrants. The oldest US trail race is the Dipsea, which began on 19 November 1905 with over 100 registered racers, and it is still going. It is now a 7.4-mile race along a breathtaking course, both in terms of the scenery and gruelling elevation, climbing three flights of stairs 'as tall as fifty-storey buildings'.

FASCINATING FACT

The Dipsea Demon Jack Kirk ran the race every year between 1930 and 2003, winning it on two occasions. Jack passed away in January 2007 at the age of 100, no doubt with his well-worn trail shoes right next to him.

The first Trans-American Footrace started on the 4 March 1928, with 199 people trying to run 3,422 miles between the Ascot Speedway, Los Angeles, and Madison Square Garden, New York, for a prize of $25,000 – more than 16 times the average income at the time. Fifty-five would finish, with the winner, Andy Payne, crossing the line after 573 hours, 4 minutes and 34 seconds. Repeated in 1929, the race length was extended to 3,553.6 miles and was won by Finnish-born Johnny Salo in an elapsed time of 525 hours, 57 minutes and 20 seconds, just two minutes and 47 seconds ahead of second place Englishman, Pietro 'Peter' Gavuzzi. Daily mileage was often over 60 with the highest being 79.9 miles. Phew.

THE TEN OLDEST AMERICAN FOOTRACES

Rank	Race	Date started	Where
1	YMCA Turkey Trot 8 km	Nov 1896	Buffalo, New York
2	Boston Marathon	Apr 1897	Boston, Massachusetts
3	Jackson Day 9 km	Jan 1907	New Orleans, Louisiana
4	Yonkers Marathon	Sept 1907	New York
5	New Orleans Turkey Day 5 mile	Nov 1907	New Orleans, Louisiana
6	Run for the Diamonds 9 mile	Nov 1908	Berwick, Pennsylvania
7	Thanksgiving Day 10 k	Nov 1908	Cincinnati, Ohio

8	YMCA Thanksgiving Day 5 mile	Nov 1908*	Poughkeepsie, New York
9	Bay to Breakers	May 1912	San Francisco
10	Lexington Patriots Day 5 mile	Apr 1914	Lexington, Massachusetts

*This footrace ended in 2007.

In 1970, the Big Apple staged its first marathon with 127 runners paying a $1 entry fee, including one woman. Fifty-five of the intrepid gathering finished, spearheading a people's running revolution, which spread to almost every corner of the globe. When Fred Lebow organised that first race, it's doubtful he could have foreseen the millions worldwide who would subsequently take up the call to legs with such gusto.

At the end of that first race just 43.3 per cent of the field ran the distance. Numbers steadily increased in the following years and by the late 1970s running was no longer seen as a preserve for elite athletes and club runners. In 2011 there were 46,795 finishers which, at the time, was a record-breaking number. In 2013, there were 50,266. By 2014, when entry numbers would have been beyond Fred's wildest expectations, the number of official finishers had risen to 50,530 out of 50,896 starters – a staggering 99.2 per cent of participants. What makes it more remarkable was that 2014 was also the year with the most first-time participants to date. From the first race in 1970 to the one which took place in 2015, the total distance run by all finishers combined equals 112 trips to the moon, or 1,074 times around the world. The descendants of Adi Dassler and running footwear manufacturers the world over owe a lot to Fred and those whom he inspired, such as Chris Brasher and John Disley: the driving forces behind the London Marathon.

The boom led to exercise disciples such as Jim Fixx. His first book, *The Complete Book of Running*, was published in 1977, stayed at the top of the bestsellers list for two years and sold over a million copies, making him the go-to running guru of the decade. His status was cemented with *Jim Fixx's Second Book of Running*. Unfortunately for Jim, he died of a heart attack whilst out running, aged just 52. The anti-running crowd had a field day at the irony of his death, although what was actually a degenerative heart condition could just have easily hit on a Saturday night in front of *Kojak*. His books are still on sale to this day – a popular tool amongst runners the world over – answering the detective's infamous line, 'Who loves ya, baby?'

THE CURRENT STATE OF AFFAIRS

By the time of Fixx's premature passing, running as a recreational pastime was firmly established. Throughout the 1980s, many half and full marathons were created all over the world, including the London Marathon and the Great North Run in the UK in 1981. It became de rigueur for any big city of note to have a major road race, dipping into the seemingly

bottomless pockets of the new wave of runners in search of adventure and travel.

In 1986, the Bay to Breakers 12.01-km/7.46-mile race was accredited by the Guinness World Records as the largest footrace ever, with over 110,000 starters, until it was surpassed by the 10.10.10 Run for the Pasig River in the Philippines with 116,086 finishers. Even that was surpassed in 2012 by the Kahit Isang Araw Lang Unity Run in the Philippines with over 209,000 participants recorded. The Bay to Breakers race remains the site for the World Centipede Running Championships and venue for numerous world record attempts before, during and after the race, including the longest one-armed conga line and the most selfies taken with race finishers.

The New York City Marathon continues to beat its own record entry year on year and the accomplishments are likely to be extended in years to come. Whilst average race times are down on those of the flared-trousers era, participation in races is significantly higher with many races being sold out within hours of their opening.

The spread of the non-professional running phenomena shows no signs of abating. A cursory glance at *Runner's World* (RW) reveals some form of race every single weekend in the UK and these continue to evolve to meet the differing needs of the thousands of runners who take part in them. Following a second running boom in the 1990s, RW expanded internationally and is now sold in countries including Argentina, Brazil, Mexico, Sweden and Turkey, supporting the growth of running all around the planet. Whatever form of running experience you are looking for and wherever that may be, it is out there – along with some you probably wouldn't even have thought about. There has never been a more exciting time for non-professional runners than right now.

FASCINATING FACT

On 28 April 2013, around 5,000 runners entered the Marathon of the North, which combined half- and full-marathon distances. Only one runner finished either race. The second- and third-placed runners lost sight of the leader Mark Hood, and went the wrong way, taking the entire field of runners with them. All were subsequently disqualified.

WHY DO WE RUN?

> *Running, one might say, is basically an absurd pastime upon which to be exhausting ourselves. But if you can find meaning in the type of running you need to do… chances are you'll be able to find meaning in that other absurd pastime – life.*
>
> **BILL BOWERMAN, COACH**

IS THERE ONE REASON?

Running means freedom, pure and simple. The 24/7 demands of modern society, emails, smartphones and social media mean for many there is little escape from work, financial worries or advertisers preaching a message that life is just not good enough without the latest must-have gadget. And that's why, in our consumer-driven society, running has never been more popular – or more important. Running is a positive way of releasing pent-up emotions. It is cheap, accessible and, apart from basic running gear, one only needs terra firma on which to run, anywhere in the world at any time. Running is pure escapism and can become addictive – if you are lucky.

THE HEALTHY OPTION

For many the number-one reason to first pull on the Lycra is health. Countless studies around the world have proven how beneficial running is in improving heart strength, facilitating weight loss and reducing blood pressure and bad cholesterol. It is one of the quickest ways to improve levels of cardiovascular fitness, especially in those runners just starting out. The fitter they become, the further and quicker they go. Those trails close to home never before ventured along will become playgrounds. Car journeys will involve new trail-spotting opportunities and noting of cemeteries with flowers – the churches tend to have outside taps, essential on a hot summer run. 'Running is my church,' said the actress Joan Van Ark, although she didn't mention plumbing.

Running improves self-esteem through weight loss, goal setting and a sense of achievement. It can help concentration, beat insomnia and even improve eyesight. It can bring new friends, adventure and travel. Ordinary Joes can dream of emulating the feats of athletic superstars like Scott Jurek and Michael Johnson, or singer David Lee Roth of Van Halen who ran the New York City Marathon in a little over six hours. Ordinary Josephines can follow in the same footsteps as Helene Diamantides, Liz Yelling or Sally Gunnell.

Sports such as bodybuilding might create a Charles Atlas-like physique, but don't go after visceral fat, which coats rather important organs. Even the dark art of cycling involves sitting down for, well, all of the time. Running, however, combines the use of large muscle groups and the need to support body weight. This helps to burn fat for up to 14 hours after an average 45-minute run because of the boost it gives to the body's metabolic rate. Combine running with friends, a trip to the seaside for a 10 k run and an extra-large Mr Whippy – once the weight is off – and life can hardly get better. For the more adventurous, follow coach Bart Yasso's example (the inventor of the Yasso 800s training technique) and race on all seven continents, or Ron Hill's and compete in races in 100 countries around the world. But Great Yarmouth is likely to be a tad cheaper.

THE RUNNER'S HIGH

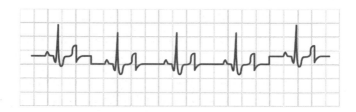

❝ *Running long and hard is an ideal antidepressant,*
since it's hard to run and feel sorry for yourself
at the same time. Also, there are those hours of
clear-headedness that follow a long run. ❞
MONTE DAVIS, RUNNER

Running can help people with mild depression and anxiety as it provides a sense of purpose, opens new horizons and gives that magic feel-good factor. Although one study reported an increase in anxiety levels in new runners, after a month many reported a marked reduction in their perceived levels of stress. Pre-running lows are swapped for post-run highs, believed by some to be caused by the production of endorphins through exercise, and by others through achieving a particular goal. Research in this area is fascinating, and some studies even discount both of these explanations. The Karolinska Institute in Sweden has suggested that through running and exercise, the body produces an enzyme called KAT that helps neutralise a harmful molecule called kynurenine, which is linked to depression. The implication is that, during exercise, muscles act in the same way as the kidneys or liver. It is even better news for triathletes; the same study found that while participation in other sports was beneficial, the most effective sports at regulating kynurenine were biking and running. Combine these two sports and the implication is that the tri brigade may benefit even more so than the runner. The study didn't consider the cost of purchasing the latest bike frame made from rhodium or CXR carbon tubular wheelsets – like the Aston Martin One-77 bicycle, a snip at $37,905. Compare that with a pair of last season's trainers at £50 from an array of online specialist retailers, and arguably running is less likely to promote the growth of the kynurenine molecule when you look at your bank balance.

Author Adharanand Finn said, 'After a run, you feel at one with the world, as though some unspecified, innate need has been fulfilled.' The average addicted mile-muncher doesn't need a medical degree to know that the runner's high is addictive, whatever the biological or physiological cause. Once achieved, a runner will want it again and again. It is an extremely exciting time in the lead-up to that first race entry, with all the fears, hopes and uncertainties it brings. It's hard to feel down when adrenaline is being produced at high levels. That addiction isn't the sole preserve of that period; as race experience takes over and the excitement of entering wanes a little, it can be replaced with the simple joy of running for no particular reason other than to run. In many ways it's like the transition from the first flushes of a relationship (where clothes are rarely on and the mention of their name will make you weak at the knees) through to enduring, satisfying, long-term love. It becomes comfortable, reassuring and an escape route – with the odd weekend of passion chucked in when you enter a race out of your comfort zone.

For many runners they just want to switch off and focus on the here and now. It's wonderfully and accurately summed up by Kate Armstrong in a fascinating piece in *Runner's World*: 'Through the years of my breakdown I yearned for the experiences that I'd had through running. Running is more than just exercise; it is a form of meditation. It was what first gave me a sense of my body. I wanted to be in the middle of a harsh landscape with the sun setting, trainers on my feet, in the lightest of clothes, knowing my body would take me safely home.' Powerful stuff, Kate.

DEATH AND RUNNER'S KNEE

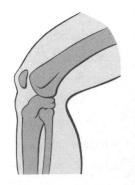

The certainties of the runner's life and reasons not to run, right? Far from it. There are high-profile cases where death and running have tragically collided, as we've seen with Fixx and Pheidippides. At the 1912 Olympic marathon in Stockholm, 20-year-old three-times Portuguese champion, Francisco Lázaro, collapsed in the race and died the next day from heatstroke. Deaths have also occurred during amateur races. But, in most cases, the act of running hasn't caused the death. Clinical studies have shown that deaths in under-35s are more likely to be due to congenital heart defects and, over that age, to heart degeneration, such as in the case of Fixx, whose pre-running obesity and heavy smoking caught up with him.

In fact, a study of over 15 years by the University of South Carolina reported a 19 per cent lower risk of death in runners compared with non-runners. For the majority, the simple act of running can extend their mobility over sedentary people by up to 16 years, increase life spans by a whopping 6.2 years for men and 5.6 years for women, and cut the risk of chronic diseases such as Alzheimer's by up to 20 per cent. While running doesn't prevent the inevitable, it can, for many, help to push it back for many years. No argument really.

FASCINATING FACT

Over the past 30 years, average marathon times have decreased in the following age brackets:

- Men aged 65–69 by an average of 15 minutes and aged 70–74 by 17 minutes

- Women aged 55–59 by 41 minutes and aged 60–64 by 16 minutes.

Non-runners invariably point to the joints of their active friends as an excuse not to take up the hobby. Injuries occur and runner's knee – or patellofemoral pain syndrome – is an occupational hazard, as are other overuse-related problems (such as the dreaded plantar fasciitis, which causes pain in the heel or bottom of the foot). In an active sport, these are to be expected, but in the longer term, runners' bone density can increase, lowering the risk of fractures. One study by the University of Missouri compared the skeletal density of runners and cyclists. It found that 63 per cent of cyclists had low mineral density in their hips and spines, compared with 19 per cent of runners. Running can also help slow the speed at which muscle mass is lost in the ageing process, even in those taking up the sport well into their seventies and eighties.

Participation in running events is on the increase among older runners whose knees seem equal to the task. Take Dave Sedgley of Ampthill and Flitwick Flyers, a septuagenarian who has run over a hundred marathons and continues to enter 100-mile challenge events. Then there is Iva Barr of Bedford Harriers, an octogenarian who first entered the London Marathon in 1982, carried the Olympic torch in 2012 and was the oldest female finisher in the 2013 London Marathon with a time of 6:37:57. In 2016, Iva started as the oldest runner and, while she wasn't able to finish, she remains an inspiration to the running community. Even Arnold Schwarzenegger has swapped at least one bench-pressing session for a bit of roadwork of late. But the relatively young muscle man will have to wait a few more years before he can challenge for the title of oldest New York male marathon finisher, which is currently held by a 93-year-old.

FASCINATING FACT

On 21 April 2013, 88-year-old Paul Freedman finished the London Marathon in a time of 7:41:33, although the record rests with Fauja Singh, who finished aged 93 in 2004. Harriette Thompson, 92, became the oldest woman to complete a marathon at the San Diego Rock'n'Roll race in 2015 in a time of 7:24:36. She had such support at the end the amazing pensioner said, 'I thought it was like Lindbergh coming in after his flight.' That will be the 1927 flight then. Wow.

WEIGHTY ISSUES

Born-again runners Neale and Emma Else previously weighed a combined 44 st 6 lb. An ordinary couple from suburbia, Neale tipped the scales at 20 st 8 lb and was heading for an early meeting with his maker – but Emma was in the lead in that race, coming in at 23 st 12 lb. The running bug took a while to grow as they struggled with gym equipment behind closed doors to lose enough weight before pounding the pavements. Neale began running at night when he thought no one was around. At that stage, it was just a means to an end and not the all-encompassing lifestyle that either of them could have contemplated would happen. As Neale says, 'I used to watch the London Marathon with envy and think that I could never run for so long. How wrong was I? I run to train and I run for fun and I run to enjoy a beer and a curry without feeling guilty.' In less than two years, Emma dropped to 9 st 12 lb and Neale to 13 st 7 lb. Both are now accomplished runners and have completed various race distances; Neale has run four marathons with a personal best time of four hours and 20 minutes to date, and Emma has run two marathons with a PB dipping under the five-hour barrier. Not content with such amazing achievements they both stepped up to run an ultramarathon while Neale embarked on a year-long daily running streak. Running has brought the pair even closer as a couple and given them a shared goal. Even having to buy multiple pairs of training shoes and the never-ending washing machine cycles to clean all their kit hasn't dampened their enthusiasm. Their healthy obsession with the sport appears to know no bounds, with Emma having permanently inked her new motto on herself. 'Hold back the dark and go further 26.2' is displayed in an artful design, and it combines her love of pop band Don Broco and running. She's hoping that Neale doesn't follow suit, given his propensity to listen to Gothic Rock.

FASCINATING FACT

A commonly held runner's view is that for every pound of weight lost, two seconds per mile are saved in a marathon; 10 lb lost can mean that a runner is more than a minute quicker in a 5 k run and more than nine minutes in a marathon. The theory works for many.

Wil Graham, a contestant on the reality television show *The Biggest Loser,* lost 8 st 7 lb to win the show, eventually going from 29 st 6 lb to under 15 st. Along the way, he discovered a love of running and bagged a half-marathon time of two hours and 20 minutes at Reading in 2011. He needed to lose weight before he could run, but after having done so he used the sport to stop the pounds from piling back on. Graham discovered that running isn't a chore, or something to be undertaken for a specific goal and then forgotten. For these people and many more like them, running has changed their lives, provided new challenges and delayed them reaching the ultimate finishing line. That's one timing mat they are happy not to cross.

MORE SEX, PLEASE, WE'RE BRITISH

" *Running is my lover.* **"**
TOSHIHIKO SEKO, ATHLETE

To London Marathon winners running might be their lover, but to other people running can improve their sexual health: for men, it's great for vascular health, impotence and erectile dysfunction, particularly in the over-50 age bracket according to one Harvard study. *The Journal of Sexual Medicine* concurs with one study which finds that inactive men are 71 per cent more likely to suffer from the last problem, in particular. For women, it's even better news. Israeli physician Alexander Olshanietzky said before the 1996 Olympics, 'Women get better results in sports competition after orgasm… the more orgasms, the more chances of winning a medal.' Lynn Jennings, US Olympic runner clearly took the advice to heart: 'sex the night before solidifies my core feelings of happiness,' she says. And she has a point. Pre-race nights can be an anxious time for many competitors, and a little canoodling might help a runner relax and get a good night's sleep.

A recent Oxford University study of 2,000 London Marathon runners concluded that those who were sexually active the night before ran an average of five minutes quicker than the abstainers (although it's entirely possible that the faster runners would have run the same time if they had also practised a little self-restraint). Furthermore, in a more recent study of one (not yet widely reported), Ian Flint noted a marked improvement in his half marathon personal best time following a night of passion. In the name of science, he intends to keep a diary to see if the consequential sleep deprivation counteracts the benefits – a risk he believes that is worth taking. Clearly a wider clinical study is needed; it is unlikely to be short of volunteers.

Boxer Rocky Balboa's coach might have told the champ, 'Women weaken the legs', but it's debatable how many athletes follow that advice the night before a big race. Who's right? No idea, but it's fun trying to find out.

TRAINING

∙∙

❝ Now, here, you see, it takes all the running you can do, to keep in the same place. If you want to get somewhere else, you must run at least twice as fast as that! ❞
LEWIS CARROLL, *THROUGH THE LOOKING-GLASS* (1872)

THE TORTOISE AND THE HARE

Beginners have to walk before they can run. Every top-class athlete started as a new runner once. Wayde van Niekerk or Wang Junxia didn't fall into a pair of spikes and become world-beaters. They began slowly, and gradually built up their ability to run longer and faster over the years. At its very essence, running for beginners and pros alike is exactly the same. It is as simple as propelling yourself along tarmac, trail or synthetic track at an increasing pace and distance. A world-class athlete in a parkrun covers the same distance as the runner coming in last and they quite literally follow the same path. New runners can make the mistake of comparing themselves to other runners when all they should be doing is running to the best of their own ability and running for themselves. With time, perseverance and sensible training, fitness levels will increase and a runner's horizons will change. A perfect goal for a new runner is to reach the point where they can run a 5 k race without stopping, irrespective of time. It is a challenging but achievable distance.

There is little benefit in telling a new runner that their aim is to run a marathon. The distance will be so far off what they see as being possible that motivation is likely to evaporate quickly. However, give a new runner a realistic goal and they can build to it sensibly, slowly and in a way that is more likely to keep them in the sport in the long term.

Trail running and a slower pace go together like Ant and Dec, although on trails it doesn't matter which side you are on. A solo run with just your thoughts for company and watching the sunrise in the gentle warmth of an early summer's morning is hard to beat. Go too fast and you may miss that rare moment of solitude in a busy day, the animals wandering back home after a night foraging, or the ones that are popping out for a spot of breakfast. Far better to see wildlife such as foxes, badgers, deer or boars in their natural habitat rather than cooped up behind a fence in a zoo.

TO PLAN OR NOT TO PLAN?

Herb Elliott had the guidance of Percy Cerutty, Paula Radcliffe had Gary Lough and Mo Farah has Alberto Salazar. Recreational runners don't have the luxury of one-to-one mentors. Nevertheless, copying the training plans of the pros could be beneficial for any runner. The pros gradually increase their training over a year with a period of base strengthening work, picking times to peak, following basic training methods and building in recovery periods.

Unless you are on a daily running streak that began on 20 December 1964 like Ron Hill, rest is as crucial to progression as the training techniques below. Training plans can be downloaded from the internet and adapted to ordinary runners' lives; long training runs in the dark can be fitted in before a day's work, for instance. No matter if it's a 5 k race, marathon or simply running to get fitter, following a structured training regime could reap rewards.

Training should be varied, involving different types of sessions and running speeds. Athletes aim for only two or three hard sessions each week, mixing slower-paced recovery runs in between.

BASIC TRAINING SESSIONS

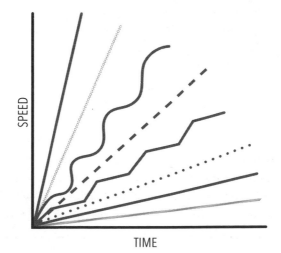

SPEED

TIME

1. **Fartleks** – rather than being a reference to Nordic flatulence, the Swedish word meaning 'speed play' is a non-rigid training device created by coach Gösta Holmér for world-class runners like Gunder Hägg and Arne Andersson. Running speed is altered over varying distances, and the objective is to run faster in short repeated bursts. The fitter the athlete, the more repetitions they will undertake.

2. **Tempos (aka lactate threshold or threshold runs)** – runs of two miles (3.2 km) or more at a pace where conversation is only just manageable. This develops an overall faster base pace as metabolic fitness is improved and the body adapts to using oxygen more efficiently. Everyone from a parkrunner to an ultrateer will benefit from a true tempo session. The session was popularised by coach Jack Daniels and, given that he has a PhD in exercise physiology, I'd say he's worth listening to.

3. **Repetitions with intervals** – another form of speed training in which intensity is near to maximum over short periods of three to five minutes. A typical session involves three minutes of hard running, with a recovery of half the effort, repeated perhaps six to eight times. These will raise a runner's lactic threshold.

4. **LSD** – not an illicit hallucinogenic substance, the initials stand for 'long slow distance'. Although it's a foundation stone for runners of any distance, it is the number-one training tool for long-distance bods in particular. Praised as the best running coach of all time by *Runner's World*, New Zealander Arthur Lydiard believed in base-building endurance through repeated LSD runs. He would insist that his athletes covered at least 100 miles (161 km) a week in training, even for 800 m runners such as Peter Snell who won gold at the 1960 Rome and 1964 Tokyo Olympics.

5. **Progression runs** – these aim to cover a specified distance while increasing the pace at different points. A runner trying to break three hours for a marathon might cover an 18-mile training run

as follows: miles one–ten at an eight-minute-mile pace, miles eleven–fourteen at a 7.5-minute pace and miles fourteen–eighteen at a seven-minute pace (close to actual race pace of six minutes and 52 seconds). The aim is to replicate race pace – or close to it – at the end of a run when legs are tired without having to run the whole distance at that pace. This allows intensive training to continue the following week. For shorter distances, another option is to head out to a turnaround point and aim to make it back to the start in a time quicker than the outward leg. Alternatively, a six-mile run could be split into three segments, or a 12-miler into four segments; whatever combination fits the plan.

6. **Hill repetitions** – a variation on the above with, yep, you guessed it, hills in the mix. These are essential for building running-specific leg strength, improving running economy, increasing fitness levels and reducing the potential for injury, as well as providing a tough workout in a short space of time.

7. **Pyramid runs** – these don't involve travelling a long way to run up the side of Khufu at Giza or El Castillo in Mexico. These are sessions with a broad base that shrink to a pinnacle and build back up again. A typical session would involve running for five minutes, pausing for two and a half minutes (i.e. half the time you've just run), running for four minutes, pausing for two minutes, running for three minutes, pausing for 90 seconds, running for two minutes and then pausing for one minute, before building back up the same way until you are running for five minutes again. Alternatively, start at one minute and build up and down the other way. The pace should increase the shorter the time.

8. **Slow, steady runs** – critical to keep you in love with the sport, they are best run with a few friends, chewing the fat and putting the world to rights.

NHS *COUCH TO 5 k* PLAN

There are lots of *Couch to 5 k* schedules available for free online, which are aimed at encouraging non-runners, or those returning from longer-term injury, to achieve a level of fitness that allows them to run an achievable distance. Beginners looking to cover that distance should find one, stick with it and build gradually to the end goal, which might be a parkrun.

Week	Run	Walk	Repeat
1	1 minute	90 seconds	8
2	2 minutes	90 seconds	6
3	3 minutes	1 minute	6
4	5 minutes	90 seconds	4
5	7 minutes	90 seconds	3
6	12 minutes	2 minutes	2
7	15 minutes	1 minute	2
8	30 minutes	N/A	1

Each of the above sessions should be repeated three times in each designated week. Given that *Runner's World* recently reported that 47 per cent of British people surveyed thought they couldn't run half a mile, the plan above has to be adapted to your own individual circumstances and used as a basic framework. Rest days are important, and a bit of weight-bearing cross training on a bike or in the pool will help if you have the time.

Training isn't about hitting each run as hard as you can every time you lace up your running shoes. Such an approach will almost inevitably lead to injury, motivational issues or potential burn out. A seasoned runner will mix up their regime in terms of the type of training sessions they undertake and their venue, and will not be afraid to run slowly. Point of fact, including at least one slower training run each week is critical for longevity and a running career lasting into later life. Ideally that slow run should be off-road and on soft ground, with the aim of starting slowly and getting slower.

There is beauty in running slowly. But there is also an addictive pleasure in running as fast as your lactic acid flooded legs will allow, heart pounding with an ever-increasing rhythmic beat, breathing laboured and intense. Running at the top end of your threshold can bring with it pain and ecstasy in equal measure. For that brief passing moment, it doesn't matter that you are never likely to run as fast as Farah or Radcliffe, or that you may never win a race. Running is about you and no one else. It is about leaving behind domesticity, your boss or even on occasions your family. It is escapism at its highest, and training at either end of the spectrum can bring with it different rewards. On a slow meandering training run you can fantasise that you are crossing the line in an Olympic final, arms aloft, taking in the roar of the crowd. On a fast training run, you can pretend that Galen Rupp is yards behind you and that if you can just keep up that last surge, he won't pass. According to Alex Gaskarth, 'dreams don't always have to exist while the sun is down and your eyes are shut.' He is entirely right.

TRAIN LIKE A PRO

There is no secret to training like a Kenyan or to running like Mo Farah, whose coach, Alberto Salazar, was himself a world-class athlete and winner of many races, including the New York and Boston marathons. Alberto has published his list of ten golden running rules, which are freely available online. Chief among these ten commandments was the advice to be consistent, take recovery runs seriously and to stay on the trail. Salazar's athletes run 90 per cent of their training sessions on soft surfaces such as trails or track, and he is an advocate of avoiding concrete as much as possible. The average amateur may not reach the point where they can run as fast or as far as professional runners, but there is no reason why they cannot adapt the pro's training methods to fit their own regime.

The difference between the pros and the rest of us is that they have the time to be totally dedicated to their sport and have access to top-level support. Runners need to be dedicated, a little selfish at times and consistent with their training plans. They should aim for achievable goals and not let life's curve balls get in their way. These simple principles are at the core of many professional athletes' training philosophies. Non-professionals have to squeeze in their running around work, school trips, shopping and countless other essential but mundane activities. Seasoned amateurs will adopt their training to life's pressures perhaps by fitting in an eight-miler on the way to work, by getting off the train a stop or two early, running the long way round to the fish and chip shop for that Friday night treat, or fitting in a lunchtime fartlek session. They may also encourage their partner to try out running in the hope that they too will be hooked and, with time, become more empathetic to the cause. Far better, when the alarm goes off at 5.45 a.m, to have a supportive partner whose reaction isn't 'really?' but 'have a good run'. With any luck, they will join you as well.

THIRTY-HOUR DAY

The biggest challenge for many amateur runners is how to fit it in every day. Adharanand Finn asked this question of one of Japan's most famous amateur runners Yuki Kawauchi, who is known as the 'citizen runner' as he works full-time. His answer was that on normal weekdays, he gets up at 7.00 a.m. trains for 90–120 minutes, goes into the office at 12.45 p.m. and works until 9.30 p.m. Given that Kawauchi's marathon PB is 2:08:14, and that this is his daily training regime, it's a wonder that he hasn't turned professional. The fact that he hasn't has made him famous in Japan. However, amateur athletes who are aiming to cover a 5 k in a new personal best time, or maybe dip under two hours for a half marathon, don't need to go to the extremes of Kawauchi's training.

RACE TRAINING

If you are training for a longer race, try entering shorter warm-up races and not running them as fast as you can. If you are training for a marathon, enter a 10 k and run the course three times. The first immediately before the race, then during and finally another lap immediately after completing the 10 k race itself (although you might attract a few odd looks as you line up sweating profusely, red faced and telling any running acquaintance in the vicinity in a slightly louder-than-needed voice that you have already run the course and as a result you are going to run a little slower today). The lap before the race when you're raring to go will fly by. Come the race itself, the benefits will include traffic control, supportive marshals, water stations, other runners and spectators which will keep your mind occupied and prevent you from concentrating on the miles ahead. The last loop is all about mental toughness and training both the mind and the body to cope with the rigours of long-distance running. The same principles can be applied to shorter distances. If you're training for a half marathon, incorporate a parkrun, or for a 10 k try adding on a mile or two beforehand.

However, don't enter a point-to-point race, reach the end and then retrace your steps along the race route. Constant cries of 'you're going the wrong way' from spectators and runners alike will become irritating, and shouts of 'show off' slightly embarrassing.

WHY DO WE RACE?

Many of us don't race, of course, but an ever-increasing number of us do as the stats in this book confirm. A professional may make their living out of racing, but why do amateurs turn up week in and week out knowing they're unlikely to win, particularly those at the back of the pack? Running has to come before racing, but does the latter ever take over?

Every racer has had a poor event at one time or not quite achieved what they were aiming for – even the greats like Paula Radcliffe, one of the world's best ever athletes. She never achieved her Olympic dreams and had some disastrous runs including Athens in 2004, when she suffered terrible stomach related issues and had to pull out of the race. She bounced back and went on to other race victories, and having the advantages of a professional support team no doubt helped. But the only reason she was able to slip back into her race shoes was that she loved running and that came before racing.

Racing creates a dichotomy. You want to enjoy it but it hurts when you reach a threshold where your mind and body must concentrate just to put one foot in front of the other and stagger the last few leg-sapping, heart-pounding miles. Even if you beat a personal best, the feeling of achievement can last a fleeting moment before the next all-out assault is planned.

For some, the reason to race is for the rare scintillating, addictive moments when training and racing come together, when your legs feel light, your stride pattern easy and your breathing aligns with a level of speed beyond what's been achieved in training. Sometimes it doesn't hit a runner until after an event, when they look back and ask themselves if they really did just achieve what they did? For others, the comfort of performing consistently week in and week out is just as valid. There are medal hunters who target specific races in order to secure an age-related win or prize, and there are runners who want to push their own perceived boundaries.

But there is no single reason why we race. Every runner will have their own, and what may work for one may not work for another. All you need to do is find the reason that works for you. Scott Jurek elegantly captured the essence of why he ran when he wrote in his book, *Eat and Run*: 'what I was often chasing was a state of mind – a place where worries that seemed monumental melted away.' As good a reason as any in my book.

WHICH TWITCHER ARE YOU?

Everyone's a twitcher. Long-distance runners need slow-twitch muscle fibres, which are good for endurance; sprinters need fast-twitch fibres designed for explosive, rapid action, which tire quickly. By the end of a 100 m race, even Usain Bolt is slowing down. He just slows down a little less quickly than the others around him. Whilst scientists believe a small percentage of the body's fibres can be trained, an athlete's muscle fibre is mainly genetically inherited. This is one of the factors that might help explain why peoples such as the Tarahumara or athletes in East Africa do well at distance running, while many sprinters can trace their lineage to West Africa whose people were spread across the globe by the slave trade.

THE BASIC ESSENTIALS

..

> ❝ *I run to breathe the fresh air... to explore... to escape the ordinary... to savour the trip along the way.* ❞
>
> **DEAN KARNAZES, ULTRAMARATHON LIVING LEGEND**

THE HEART OF THE MATTER

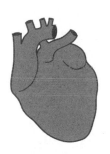

When running, the heart increases the number of beats over its resting rate as the body absorbs oxygen into the blood. Runners benefit from increased cardiac output, which is the amount of oxygen-rich blood that travels from the heart, through tiny capillaries to the muscles. The more the heart is able to pump, the less it is strained. Regular, consistent training can help develop a stronger heart when combined with changes in lifestyle, such as giving up a pre-existing nicotine habit or changing a diet rich in saturated fatty foods. Trained athletes usually have significantly lower resting heart rates than the wider population. While that isn't a guarantee against heart problems, it puts a runner on the right side of the risk divide. In the 1980 Moscow Olympics, runner Sebastian Coe was rumoured to have a resting heartbeat of 28 bpm and a sustained heart rate of 250 bpm when running. Compare that with a healthy adult whose bpm is in the 60–80 range and it's no wonder he won gold.

SLEEP

Tired people can crave chocolate or other fatty foods high in the kind of content that runners should avoid. Less than six hours of sleep per night means that the body is likely to produce increased levels of the hunger hormone, ghrelin, and cause other harmful biological reactions. A bad night's sleep followed by a stressful day increases the chances of a runner reaching for the cookie jar rather than a leafy salad, and this is a view supported by extensive studies. One such study found that its tired test subjects, who were shown a picture of food high in fat and carbohydrates, had a higher response reaction in the 'reward centre' of their brains compared with those that were shown pictures of healthier options.

Lack of good quality sleep also affects muscle, cartilage and bone repair, as it inhibits growth hormone (GH), a small, powerful protein made by the pituitary gland released into the bloodstream. The production of GH is essential to help turn all those training miles into real fitness gains. The more we sleep, the higher the GH production and the better athletic performance, which is why some athletes turn to GH injections. This practice has been banned by a wide variety of sporting authorities including the

Olympic committee in 1989 and the World Anti-Doping Agency. All athletes can beat the cheats by powering down their laptops and televisions an hour or so before they want to nod off, avoiding late night cappuccinos, and easing into a good book to try to ensure a full, uninterrupted night's sleep.

> ❝ No one tires of dreaming, because to dream is to forget, and forgetting does not weigh on us, it is a dreamless sleep throughout which we remain awake. In dreams I have achieved everything. ❞
>
> **FERNANDO PESSOA, *THE BOOK OF DISQUIET***

Ideally, runners should aim to clock eight to ten hours' shut-eye in order to maintain a good metabolic rate, to allow the body to repair, and still have time to dream of standing on the winners' podium, flag raised and national anthem being sung. It will help you maintain attention the next day and therefore to train better: your perceived exertion effort on a training run is more likely to be accurate, so in turn may spur you on a tad quicker or further. A runner coming into a training session tired and a little grumpy is more likely to feel the effort is too hard or not put as much into it, compared with the same runner the next day in the same session who has a full and restorative night's sleep. So, to become a better runner, sleep more and follow Fernando's advice.

FRINGE BENEFITS

Professional athletes like Kílian Jornet Burgada can eat whatever and whenever they want: if you are running 140 miles

(225 km) a week and entering ultras all over the world it's not a problem. For the weekend athlete, however, it is. Running isn't a passport to weight loss and deep-fried Mars Bars (they do exist and taste lovely). If the aim is to shed a few pounds, a runner should avoid too many high-calorie sports drinks or fatty foods. Fish and chips might have worked for comic book running legend Alf Tupper and his Greystone Harriers pals, but it's unlikely to work for other aspiring 'toughs of the track' if every run is rewarded with a high-calorie treat.

When body mass is reduced, VO_2 max is increased. This is the amount of oxygen consumed per kilogram of body weight. The lighter the runner, the further and faster they are likely to go. The impact pressure on muscles, joints and the body generally lessens, and the risk of injury lowers. So, the bad news is that to get speedy the fry-ups have to be shelved. The good news is that another study found a 45-minute workout could boost metabolic rate for up to 14 hours. That's not to say a blowout shouldn't happen. On the contrary – life is for living and when a particular race has been run, or a milestone reached, being able to tuck into a guilt-free slice of something naughty is nigh on mandatory.

TEN BASIC NUTRITION RUNNING TIPS

1. Never eat anything new on race day or in the lead-up to an event or long training run.
2. Practise race-fuelling in training, both in terms of drink and any food or gels that will be consumed during a race.

3. When going on any long-distance training run, keep hydrated but don't drink too much fluid (see Hyponatremia, p.58)

4. Avoid drinking too much caffeine, fizzy drinks with extra sugar, and too much amber nectar.

5. Eat sensibly and well both during training and in the immediate lead-up to the race, keeping your meals balanced with the following:
   - Carbohydrates – found in wholegrain pasta, rice, potatoes and starchy vegetables (avoid white bread, pastries and highly processed food);
   - Protein – lean meats, poultry, beans and wholegrains (avoid food sources that come with a high saturated-fat content);
   - Calcium – plain yoghurt, soy milk, tofu, salmon;
   - Essential fats – edamame, nuts, oil, kidney beans and flaxseeds.

6. The night before a race have a meal low in fat and high in carbohydrate with a moderate amount of protein, and don't overeat.

7. Use race morning breakfast to top up glycogen stores. Aim for about 0.5 g of carbohydrate per pound of body weight for every hour before the race. For example, if you weigh 13 st, aim for around 130 g of carbohydrates two hours or so before the race starts.

8. Don't eat food with more than five ingredients as it is more likely to be processed.

9. Avoid foods with added sugar (studies have linked this with the development of degenerative disorders) and foods marked low fat or light, as these often have added sugar.

10. If you want to run well, cut down on alcohol use. If possible, eliminate it in the month before a race, and certainly in the week before a race.

There are many contradictory studies on what an athlete should eat and drink. For example, a study will come out extolling the virtues of eating red meat and drinking wine; the following week another warns of impending doom if you ingest the same stuff. Even the so-called experts can change their views over what is right or wrong. Take the case of Tim Noakes, a South African runner, Emeritus Professor in Exercise Science and Sports Medicine, and the author of the apparently definitive study on the relationship between science and running, *The Lore of Running* (LOR). Published in 1985, LOR became known as the distance runner's bible. His dietary advice, which extolled the virtues of a high carbohydrate/low fat diet for athletes, shaped what runners ate for two generations. LOR was the athletic equivalent to the *Haynes Manual*. Then, suddenly, he said that he got it wrong and that if anyone had the LOR they should 'tear out the section on nutrition'. Noakes is now advocating the opposite, insisting that runners should ingest low quantities of carbohydrates and high quantities of fats. If such a well-known, highly respected and professionally qualified figure like Noakes can say that we should discount his advice and follow new advice, it's no wonder that nutrition continues to be a hot topic. It's almost enough to reach for a non-nutritious chocolate bar of the same name.

TOP RUNNING TIPS FROM EXPERIENCED RUNNERS

- Have clean, fresh socks in a backpack or car; you can't beat the feeling of changing them after a long run, especially if it's been wet and muddy

- If you're running in a tight T-shirt then consider wearing nipple guards
- Take sandals with you to wear after a race or long run
- Well-fitting pants are just as important as sports bras
- Wear a decent pair of gloves in freezing winter months or else you may not get back into the car
- Wear running gear that fits you, not what looks good in a catalogue
- Pick races with free buffets at the end for immediate recovery
- During races, look at the vests around you to see if you're running with half or full marathoners as that will affect your pace
- A couple of Imodium before a long race might avoid those number two moments
- Tell someone where you are going
- Acknowledge other runners
- Don't leave damp training shoes on the front seat of a car in hot conditions all day
- Laugh at roadside hecklers internally to avoid a confrontation
- Plan training runs past churches, pubs or halls with outside water taps
- Pack your running kit the night before a race and check it twice
- Run against the flow of traffic
- Enter LDWA (Long Distance Walkers Association) races as they provide superb value
- Leave extra cash in race holdalls for forgotten running kit
- Leave water bottles en route and collect them afterwards

HYPONATREMIA

The advice on how much fluid to drink has also changed significantly within a short period. Originally, runners were advised to take on fluid at a high rate in the lead-up to an event, and during the race itself, to take it on board early, frequently and at a rate that would be sufficient to replace water in the body lost through sweat. Prevailing advice was that thirst was not a good indicator of whether fluid was needed and, if you had reached that stage, you were already dehydrated and in trouble. In recent years, however, there have been increased reports of runners suffering from hyponatremia, a condition that occurs when the amount of sodium in a person's blood drops below a safe level. The faster and quicker sodium levels drop the more dangerous it can become. In athletics terms, this can be caused through a combination of excessive fluid intake and sodium being lost through sweating. The condition is reported to have led to deaths, particularly in marathons, so it is well worth following government guidelines. Organisations such as the American College of Sports Medicine now believe that the dangers of over-hydration outweigh those of under-hydration, and the International Marathon Medical Directors Association recommends drinking in relation to thirst. Tim Noakes, in his book *Waterlogged*, also advocates the same advice and suggests consuming no more than 800 ml per hour.

GEAR AND GADGETS

....

> *A Dandy is a Clothes wearing Man,*
> *a Man whose trade, office and existence*
> *consists in the wearing of Clothes.*
>
> **THOMAS CARLYLE, *SARTOR RESARTUS***

GEAR AND GADGETS ARE ESSENTIAL, RIGHT?

Flying legal eagle Adam Campbell gained an unofficial world record for running the fastest marathon in a suit in a time of 2:35:51 at Canada's Victoria Marathon in 2012. Unfortunately for Adam, he failed to register with Guinness World Records, who officially hold Joe Elliot's 2013 time of 2:58:03 as the current benchmark. Not known for their wicking propensities, a three piece is not the athletic clothing of choice for most. Modern sports technology has led to major advances in the type of clothing and running-related gadgets that are available to recreational and professional athletes alike. Absorbent materials like cotton – which becomes heavy, wet and clingy with perspiration – have been replaced with synthetic materials that help moisture evaporate quicker, although can still lead to runner's nipple without a liberal coating of Vaseline.

A well-known photograph of Dorando Pietri being helped across the finishing line of the 1908 Olympic marathon shows him wearing baggy clothing. Now, compression clothing for almost every part of the body has been developed. Satellite navigation watches, nutrition bars, gels, miniature personal music devices, smartphones with downloadable applications and all manner of paraphernalia including bumbags, hydration rucksacks, Anti Monkey Butt Powder to avoid chafing and Shewees are now in many sports bags. It's a wonder how Pietri ever made it across the finish line. (Oh, that's right, he was helped and disqualified.)

FASCINATING FACT

Keith Levasseur ran Baltimore Marathon in 2012 in a time of 2:46:58 wearing flip-flops, earning himself a Guinness World Record. Other world records include Sarah Dudgeon, who ran the London Marathon in 2015 wearing a wedding dress in 3:16:44. In 2016, Lee Goodwin crossed the finish line in 3:02:43 dressed as a flower pot, Kate Godof (3:15:39) dressed as a tortoise and Dave Cooke (5:45:51) dressed in chainmail.

TO SHOE OR NOT TO SHOE - BLESS YOU

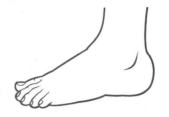

Homo erectus was the pioneer of the barefoot running craze long before Abebe Bikila won the Rome Olympic marathon shoeless in 1960. His world record time of 2:15:16 stood as a barefoot record until 1978 when it was beaten by India's Shivnath Singh, in Jalandhar, in a time of 2:12:00. Other shoeless devotees are athletes Bruce Tulloh, Zola Budd and the Tarahumara tribe in Mexico highlighted by Christopher McDougall in *Born to Run*. Early runners were saved a few shillings, but over the past few thousand millennia the training shoe industry has grown to an estimated £3.2 billion. The now omnipresent global sports goods titans have shoes designed to meet the complex needs of the 33 joints, 26 bones and more than 100 ligaments, muscles and tendons that make up the foot.

> **❝** *I prefer running without shoes. My toes didn't get cold. Besides, if I'm in front from the start, no one can step on them.* **❞**
> **MICHELLE DEKKERS, CROSS-COUNTRY RUNNER**

The runner is faced with a dazzling and confusing array of training shoes to meet intricate and different needs. Pronation, overpronation and supination running styles are catered for in minimalist, neutral, motion control, cushioned, barefoot or performance shoes for trail, track, road and pretty much any other surface you can think of save the moon (although that is just a matter of time). Most manufacturers change their shoes with each new athletic season, often with little obvious change to even the most committed fan other than cosmetic. The super powers know that, once within their fold, repeat business (as shoes are worn out and replaced) is as certain as death and taxes. Once the right pair of shoes is found, it takes an event of seismic proportions to persuade a runner to move away from them.

New runners should have their running gait expertly assessed and avoid buying shoes that look the best in the shop. This doesn't mean spending a fortune, but rather finding the right fit for their specific foot. A study at the University of Bern in Switzerland, published recently in *Medicine & Science in Sports & Exercise*, assessed 4,358 runners. It concluded that athletes with shoes costing more than $95 (£76), with features such as extra cushioning, were twice as likely to be injured at some point than those with shoes costing less than half. One size does not fit all.

IF THE SHOE FITS: A TIMELINE

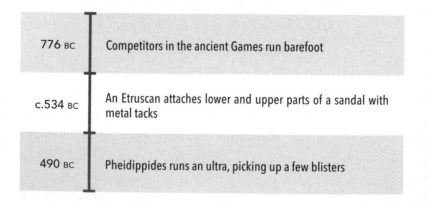

776 BC	Competitors in the ancient Games run barefoot
c.534 BC	An Etruscan attaches lower and upper parts of a sandal with metal tacks
490 BC	Pheidippides runs an ultra, picking up a few blisters

341 BC	Etruscan invention takes off
1830	An athletic shoe made from canvas and rubber is invented
1832	Wait Webster patents a design attaching rubber to shoes and boots (and creates the 'sneak thief', as the shoes were so quiet)
1854	Boots and shoes with spikes are developed
1870	John Boyd Dunlop invents plimsolls, later called Green Flash
1890s	Spiked running shoes sold by J. W. Foster & Sons (which later becomes Reebok)
1904	Alf Shrubb, wearing the Foster spikes, breaks three different records in one race
1916	Keds trainer called Champion created with rubber sole
1924	Foster's supply the British Olympic team, including Eric Liddell and Harold Abrahams
1936	Adi Dassler supplies shoes to Jesse Owens

FOR THE LOVE OF RUNNING

1948	Adidas formed by Adi Dassler and Puma by Rudolf Dassler
1949	Asics was born
1952	Josy Barthel wears Puma shoes to win gold in the 1,500 m at Helsinki Olympics
1955	Marty McFly time travels from 1985 wearing not yet invented Nike trainers in *Back to the Future*
1958	Reebok founded by the descendants of Joe Foster
1960	New Balance create a shoe with a wedged heel
1968	Tommie Smith wears Puma Suedes in 200 m at Mexico Olympics
1968	Smith and John Carlos remove their shoes for the medal ceremony
1971	Nike pays Carolyn Davidson $35 for her 'swoosh' design
1973	Steve Prefontaine endorses Nike and wears the company's shoes

1974	Nike launches its 'waffle' shoe design
1975	Brooks uses EVA foam to lighten its shoes
1977	Dave Starsky becomes a trend-setting television detective wearing Adidas Dragons
1980s	Training shoe sales explode and move into casual day wear
1982	Asics release the Tiger X-Caliber GT, incorporating pronation control and air flex canals which provided decent cushioning for the runner
1983	Reebok expand into free style trainers catering for the aerobics boom
1985	Asics introduces a gel cushioning system
1986	Reebok's sales rise from £1 million in 1983 to over £1 billion worldwide
1986	Adidas produce the Micropacer with an electronic pedometer in its tongue
1987	Nike create an iconic fashion trainer Air Max 1

1994	Forrest Gump runs across America in Nike Cortez originally created in 1971
2003	Paula Radcliffe smashes the women's world record with a time of 2:17:25 in the London Marathon wearing Nike
2004	Nike release the Free 5.0, a cross between barefoot and standard running shoe
2005	Vibram introduces FiveFingers shoes – mimicking barefoot running – and the rest try to catch up
2008	Haile Gebrselassie runs a new world record of 2:03:59 at the Berlin Marathon, wearing bright yellow Adidas trainers
2009	Hoka seek to reverse the minimalist trend with their One One shoe
2014	Saucony offer ProGrid cushioning, memory foam, low heel drops and more
2016	Usain Bolt runs into the history books at the Rio Olympics wearing Puma Spikes
2029	Manufacturers try to produce shoes lighter than feathers
2034	Barefoot running takes over and the circle of life starts again

SATELLITE-NAVIGATION DEVICES

One of the most important advances for runners in the past 20 years has been the availability to the mass market of good quality, portable, accurate satellite-navigation watches which can incorporate

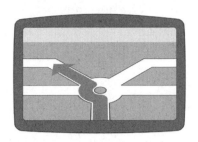

all manner of data. They record the distance run, cycled or swum, the time, average speed, route, calories burnt and heart rate, and even provide virtual running partners to race or train with. Runs can also be uploaded and shared instantly via the internet.

Garmin was one of the first companies to grab a wristhold in the watch market in 1990 and has since produced market-leading devices. The name of the company is now as synonymous with speed and distance monitors as Kleenex is with tissues. By 2010, Garmin's early, highly functional watches, which resembled small bricks, had been replaced by models such as the Garmin Forerunner 110, which looks like, well, a normal watch. Fast-forward to now and the choice on offer to the athlete can be bewildering. Garmin alone offer three different GPS-enabled models just for runners, and five for triathletes. The new kid on the block, Fitbit, tells you how long you've slept and tracks your heartbeat, steps taken, and even how many stairs you have climbed, as well as recording distance and time. It's rare to line up on a race starting line these days without seeing a number of people with one wrist held out horizontally in front and the other hand waiting in eager anticipation to push the start button.

ONLINE SUPPORT

An increasing number of athletes are turning to their computers to aid them in their training. Websites such as Strava offer the runner the opportunity to interact online with their friends and countless other runners around the world they will never met. The company describes itself as the ultimate athlete resource as it allows runners to connect to it via GPS enabled watches and smartphones. Runners can create their own virtual running community and share with it where they have gone, how fast they have run and even a map of the route they have taken. They can upload photographs and share information about routes which benefit others living close by. It also offers monthly challenges to help motivate the athlete. It is free to join although premium features do come at a monthly cost and include personalised coaching and detailed analysis. Similar applications include MapMyRun, Good Run Guide, Runtastic, WalkJogRun and Endomondo. For the braver runner, the Zombies, Run website offers a virtual running game with purportedly over one million players worldwide. The game is simple: download a mission and music which the runner listens to while out running. As the Zombies begin to catch up, pick up the pace to get away and collect supplies along the way. It's a wonder how anyone managed to find the motivation to train before smartwatches and phones.

MUSIC ON THE RUN

Rhodesian-based English runner Arthur Newton won the Comrades Marathon in Durban, South Africa, five times and set a host of records in races, including the 100-mile London to Bath race and other 24-hour events in the 1930s. His racing plans included the use of a large gramophone. Whereas a spot of swing from Satchmo might have helped Newton, for the next 40 years he would be in a minority of runners who could use music to their advantage. The Sony Walkman was the first portable personal music device to hit the masses and it transformed the way people trained. A bulky boxed cassette player strapped to the waist, it allowed a small number of songs to be listened to while running; the user could imagine they were running up the steps of the Philadelphia Museum of Art like boxer Rocky Balboa, whilst pumping out 'Eye of the Tiger' for the fourth time. The development of the iPod and other small devices now allows thousands of songs to be taken on a run.

Studies have shown that upbeat music may help a runner clock faster times as they train to the beat, block out negative thoughts and experience increased blood flow, which helps to disperse lactic acid build up. On the flipside, another study conducted over a period of six years reported a 300 per cent increase in serious injuries to pedestrians wearing headphones, so running to music is not without danger. In 2007, the New York City Marathon banned the use of headphones through fear of injuries and most major races are now following suit.

ROCKING RUNNERS

- Sean Combs (aka Puff Daddy, Diddy, P. Diddy), 2003 New York City Marathon (4:14:54)

- Flea (Red Hot Chili Peppers), 2012 Los Angeles Marathon (3:41:49)

- Nick Hexum (311), 2006 Los Angeles Marathon (5:29:44)

- Björn Ulvaeus (ABBA), 1980 Stockholm Marathon (3:23:54)

- Stuart Murdoch (Belle and Sebastian) 1986 Glasgow Marathon (2:57:08)

- Ronan Keating (Boyzone), 2008 London Marathon (3:59:44)

- Mike Malinin (Goo Goo Dolls), 2000 San Francisco Marathon (3:23:56)

- Bernard Butler (Suede) 2014 London Marathon (4:30:12)

- Alanis Morissette, 2009 Bizz Johnson Trail Marathon (4:17:03)

- David Lee Roth (Van Halen), 2010 New York City Marathon (6:04:43)

- Joe Strummer (The Clash), 1982 Paris Marathon (allegedly 3:20)

- Simon Taylor-Davis (Klaxons) 2014 London Marathon (4:20:03)

- Johnny Marr (The Smiths) 2010 New York Marathon (3:54:18)

GEAR AND GADGETS

Make running a habit. Set aside a time solely for running. Running is more fun if you don't have to rush through it.

JIM FIXX

Like the stars of *March of the Penguins*, runners can become focused on destinations and goals; they love numbers. Time, distance run, speed, elevation and descent are eagerly dissected and analysed. The target of a new personal best or finishing position in a race can detract from the joy of the journey. It's unlikely penguins on their treks will pull up and check out the views, but runners should. The use of GPS watches and the focus on the data they create can detract from the very thing an athlete enjoys in the first place, which is the simple act of pulling on their gear and heading out of the door for a run.

Watches and measurement devices play an important role in keeping the athlete honest in their ability. They should not, however, be allowed to distract you from the beauty of an early-morning cross-country run when most people are just waking up, or cause an athlete to become fixated on the numbers to the detriment of the reasons that brought them to the sport in the first place.

An advocate of running without devices was the late ultrarunner Micah True, or Caballo Blanco as he became known to the native Tarahumara tribe in Mexico, who became famous through *Born to Run*. Born Michael Randall Hickman in Oakland, California, in 1953, True championed enjoyment and the act of running itself over time and speed.

A healthy balance between the use of all the top-of-the-range gadgets and running without any could lead to longer-term

FOR THE LOVE OF RUNNING

running careers for non-professional athletes. There will inevitably be periods when motivation drops. A blast of The Rolling Stones, as favoured by Phil Hewitt in *Keep on Running*, might make the difference between a six-miler and another slice of pizza. Better still, put the miles in and have a guilt-free slice after the run. Another option is to run and eat pizza at the same time, as ultrarunning legend Dean Karnazes did at midnight on Highway 116 in Napa Valley, California, in the middle of a 150-mile plus training run. He opted for a large with all the trimmings.

RUNNING CLUBS

> ❝ *We are runners when we lace up our trainers, come rain or shine, early flight or late-night deadline.* ❞
> **SAM MURPHY, COACH**

A GENTLEMAN'S CLUB?

Running in the nineteenth and early twentieth century in Britain was divided between the professionals, who were often in low-paid employment, and the wealthy who joined exclusive 'gentleman amateur' clubs, such as the Thames Hare & Hounds where tradesmen were not welcomed. Still in existence to this day, the club remained a very conservative institution, not allowing women to enter until 1981, the year of the first London Marathon and the Great North Run.

The British running boom in the 1980s saw clubs like London-based Serpentine created in response to the new breed of runners and slew of races being created. The club was established by runners training for that year's London

Marathon. It now boasts over 2,100 members with around 42 per cent being women, and membership from all corners of the globe and walks of life.

The archaic, outdated values of the early clubs have long ago disappeared and been replaced with clubs seeking to meet the needs of all runners, no matter their gender, age or ability.

A common misconception is that running clubs are full of virile, testosterone-fuelled young alpha males and females, with lithe bodies and egos to match. But a casual observation of any local 10 k race would make it obvious that running clubs have a cross-section of membership of all abilities. Running clubs can be found in every part of the UK, some catering for specific sections of society. Northern Frontrunners are a lesbian, gay, bisexual and transgender running club; Vegan Runners UK and Christian Runners both have an obvious membership base; Fetch Everyone is an internet-based club. It's the shared love of running which unites all clubs and their members.

WHY JOIN A CLUB?

The benefits of joining a running club are many, including the following:

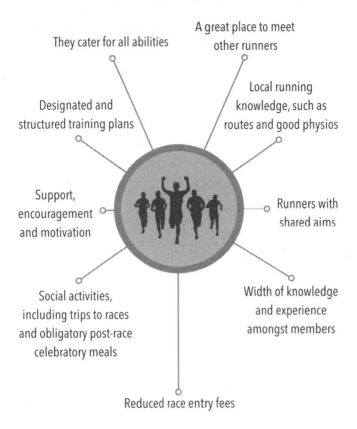

They cater for all abilities

A great place to meet other runners

Designated and structured training plans

Local running knowledge, such as routes and good physios

Support, encouragement and motivation

Runners with shared aims

Social activities, including trips to races and obligatory post-race celebratory meals

Width of knowledge and experience amongst members

Reduced race entry fees

Whilst it is not necessary to be a club member to be a runner, a new joiner might also experience a psychological shift in their perception of themselves. They may no longer see themselves as someone who runs. Instead, they are a runner; a small but important change, which can lead to self-belief, confidence and willingness to try something new.

HOW TO FIND A RUNNING CLUB

If you are based in the United Kingdom, each of the home countries have their own individual national athletic organisations, such as Welsh Athletics or Athletics Northern Ireland, which provide a wealth of information about clubs all around the country. Each offer a find-a-club service, and it's worth doing some research as not all clubs are the same. Some might offer a track-based training programme while another might focus on fell or road running. Bedford and County AC, for example, are an entirely different club to Bedford Harriers AC even though they share the same facilities. The older, well-established clubs tend to be easy to locate through a brief online search. It is the smaller, less high-profile local clubs that can be more difficult to locate. The Run Together organisation is an off-shoot of England Athletics and allows a qualified and insured run leader to set up a group and advertise its existence on the main webpage. The groups tend to be ideal for new runners or those coming back from a long-term lay-off who want to build their fitness slowly. Another option is to look at online running social media websites such as Strava or Fetch Everyone.

FETCH EVERYONE

This internet-based club records over 84,580 registered users on its website as of the start of 2017. The site provides a free service allowing runners to record what they are doing, interact with other users and complete training diaries. An extensive forum page promotes lively chat and discussion about all manner of things, not always running-related. Its members are called 'Fetchies' and wear eye-catching, colourful club gear, which makes them stand out at races and helps them to identify each other.

FASCINATING FACT

Fetch member Naomi Prasad was the first UK woman to run 100 marathons before the age of 30. She married fellow Fetchie, Mark Studdart, in 2012 having met through the site. Prasad also briefly held the title of the UK's fastest female marathon runner of the decade with a time of 4:18:49, which she ran in Zürich on New Year's Day 2010. Unfortunately, she only held the title for three weeks until her time was bettered.

THE 100 MARATHON CLUB

This is slightly more difficult to join as the UK club requires runners to have completed 100 officially measured and verifiable road or trail marathons. There are 100 Clubs all over the world, including New Zealand, Finland and Germany, some of which will allow training runs to count towards a runner's total. The stats of some of the UK club members are very impressive and include the following records (as of January 2017):

100 CLUB RECORDS (UK)

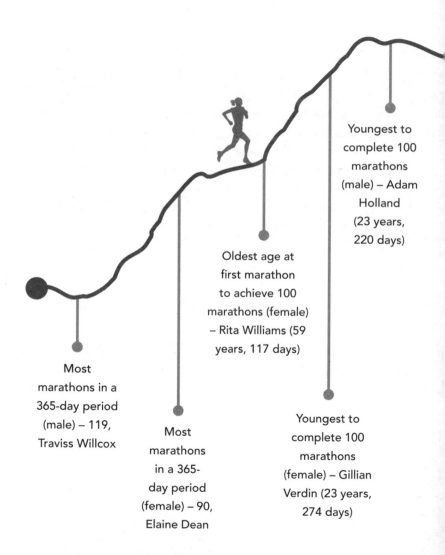

Youngest to complete 100 marathons (male) – Adam Holland (23 years, 220 days)

Oldest age at first marathon to achieve 100 marathons (female) – Rita Williams (59 years, 117 days)

Most marathons in a 365-day period (male) – 119, Traviss Willcox

Most marathons in a 365-day period (female) – 90, Elaine Dean

Youngest to complete 100 marathons (female) – Gillian Verdin (23 years, 274 days)

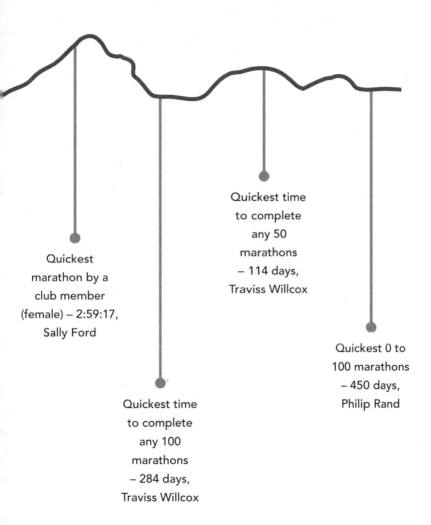

Quickest marathon by a club member (female) – 2:59:17, Sally Ford

Quickest time to complete any 100 marathons – 284 days, Traviss Willcox

Quickest time to complete any 50 marathons – 114 days, Traviss Willcox

Quickest 0 to 100 marathons – 450 days, Philip Rand

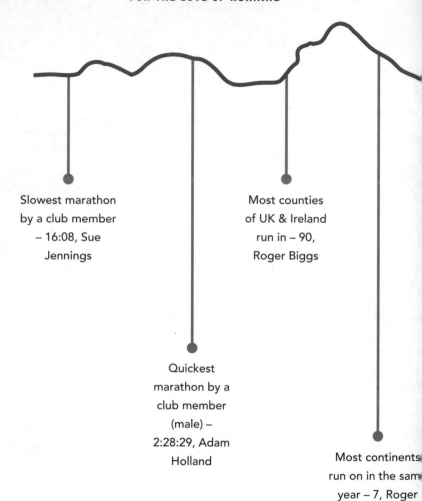

Slowest marathon by a club member – 16:08, Sue Jennings

Most counties of UK & Ireland run in – 90, Roger Biggs

Quickest marathon by a club member (male) – 2:28:29, Adam Holland

Most continents run on in the same year – 7, Roger Biggs

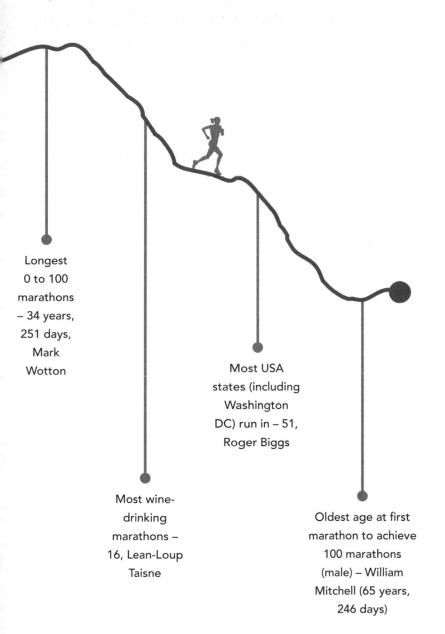

Longest 0 to 100 marathons – 34 years, 251 days, Mark Wotton

Most wine-drinking marathons – 16, Lean-Loup Taisne

Most USA states (including Washington DC) run in – 51, Roger Biggs

Oldest age at first marathon to achieve 100 marathons (male) – William Mitchell (65 years, 246 days)

THE BOB GRAHAM 24 HOUR CLUB

Membership of the Bob Graham 24 Hour Club is prized in fell-running circles. The club is open to anyone who can complete the 72-mile Bob Graham Round in less than 24 hours. Set in the Lake District, the route is named after a Keswick guesthouse owner who set the record for the quickest time in 1932, although it was broken in 1960 by Alan Heaton. Sounds easy? Factor in that the precise route covers 42 peaks, 27,000 feet of ascent and descent, and peaks including Skiddaw (3,054 ft), Bowfell (2,960 ft) and Scafell Pike (3,206 ft), and it's little wonder membership is so precious.

The club opened its tent flaps to potential peak baggers in 1960. Twenty years later, the task was so difficult membership stood at only 141. By the end of 2015, that had grown to 1,975 hardy men and women, helped by the growth of knowledge within the club of the best routes. Over the years, there have been remarkable achievements: Roger Baumeister running the round twice in 46:34:30 in 1979; Billy Bland's unfeasibly quick 13:53:00 in 1982; Jasmin Paris' 15:24 women's record in April 2016; and the winter rounds (most are in the height of summer), when light is limited and the terrain more difficult. Jasmin also nailed the winter record in February of the same year in a time of 22:08, highlighting just how difficult the ground and conditions can be. Running mile after mile through water, bogs, deep mud, on constantly undulating, rocky terrain, with the wind making it so cold you can't feel your nose or ears, and with almost overwhelming feelings of tiredness, takes a fair degree of commitment to the cause. The small band that has extended the number of peaks bagged in the same time limit are in another league. Mark Hartell's 77-peak run in 1997 in 23:47 is worthy of a chapter on its own. The fell-running legend Joss Naylor's 61, 63 and 72 peaks, the latter covering 100 miles and around 38,000 feet of ascent in the 1970s is an inspiration to all potential peak baggers. In 2016, Naylor celebrated his eightieth birthday the only way he possibly could, by running 30 miles from Caldbeck to Wasdale in the Lake District. Any prospective member would benefit from reading Richard Askwith's *Feet in the Clouds* – and then do something simpler, like run a marathon carrying a fridge. Yep, that's been done.

FASCINATING FACT

Tony Phoenix-Morrison (aka Tony the Fridge) ran Kielder Marathon with a 40-kg fridge strapped to his back, a month after running the course of the Great North Run on 30 consecutive days, including the main race. In April 2013, he also carried a 42-kg Smeg fridge around Newcastle quayside for a full 24 hours on a solo run to raise funds for the Sir Bobby Robson Foundation.

GOODGYM

The idea for the GoodGym running club, which combines getting fit and doing good for someone else, was conceived by founder Ivo Gormley. It could be as simple as running to the shops to grab a newspaper for an elderly neighbour or galvanizing a group to do something for the community, such as clearing a park of rubbish. The club's webpage encourages runners to join and take part in 'one-off missions' or commit to weekly social visits and everything in-between. It's not just a good deed club, having become affiliated in 2014 with qualified and experienced coaches. Gormley believes that the combination of running and doing something positive creates for the runner fitness gains and a 'deeper connection with your local area and with other people'.

HASH HOUSE HARRIERS

Known as the 'drinking club with a running problem', HHH was started by British Colonial officers and expatriates in Kuala Lumpur, Malaysia in 1938. It now has a network of 1,570 'chapters' in 184 countries. A typical run is usually on a Monday night and involves a hare, starting a trail five or six miles ahead of the runners, with one of the aims of the club being to run off the weekend hangovers. The hares use flour or chalk to mark the trail for a short distance and then stop, leaving open the possibility that the trailing runners may shoot off on the wrong trail. After 200 m or so, the hare will again begin marking the trail and the same process is repeated until the end of the run or the hare is caught. Faster runners might go wrong, allowing the slower runners the chance to catch up and overtake. Then it's all off to the pub, the trail to which the hare doesn't usually need to mark.

CARPE VIAM

Despite its alarming name, the Dead Runners Society doesn't require death as a qualifying joining requirement, although once in, members are 'deads'. The DRS is a worldwide virtual online running club founded by Chris Conn in Texas in 1991, merging the power of emails and, later, the internet, with sport. The aim of the club is to informally share anything running related, from meditation to marathons. It has its own flag (incorporating a running figure and smiley emoticon), race wear, terminology, annual world conferences and offshoots of the main body around the world including STiLlDEADs (St Louis Dead Runners Society), SOBER Deads (Southern Ontario and Buffalo Expired Runners) and DEADeNZ (Dead Runners New Zealand). Primarily a running community, discussion pages extend to music, parenting and the other dark art, triathlons.

THE EVER PRESENTS

This is a club that many marathoners would like to enter, although it's impossible to do so for any amount of money and, with the passage of time, its membership is shrinking. The Ever-Present club comprises 12 runners who, as of 2016, have run every London Marathon since the first race in 1981. Over the years membership has declined from 42 and, at their own admission, they 'have less hair, less teeth, less ability – however their force, dedication and perseverance is still there.' Given Chris Finill's very impressive 2:56:05, who was 57 at the time of the 2016 race and the youngest EP member, the 'less ability' statement is debatable. An even more impressive fact is that Chris has run every single marathon in a time below three hours with a PB of 2:28:27 in 1985. The oldest EP in the 2016 race was Ken Jones, a sprightly 82-year-old, who, in the early years, also clocked a couple of sub-threes, which, to many club runners, is their equivalent of climbing the Eiger. Each member has their own fascinating story to tell and a cursory glance through their records over the years provides a fascinating insight into a wide range of running careers. In 1995, the Marathon organisers recognised their status with a special medal and guaranteed each member entry to all future races.

FASCINATING FACT

Chris Finill obtained the Guinness World Record for running the most consecutive editions of the World Marathon Majors in under 3:30, between 29 March 1981 and 25 April 2010.

THE VETERANS ATHLETIC CLUB (VAC)

VAC was established in 1931 and currently admits runners over the age of 35 only, with a passport required as proof of age. It caters mainly for runners in London and the South West and, irrespective of the vet label, the club members consistently produce top-class times. It's no surprise really when you look at some of the past members which include Ron Franklin, who ran in the Melbourne Olympics in 1956, and Sir Chris Chataway, who joined in 2006 at the age of 74. Chataway was a GB Olympic runner in 1952 and 1956; he helped Bannister break the four-minute-mile barrier in 1954 and achieved a world record in the 5,000 m the same year, as well as becoming BBC's first Sports Personality of the Year. The only slightly disconcerting thing about joining the club is that it has its own obituary page for former members.

SHOULD I JOIN A CLUB?

The answer is: it's up to you. Olympian Lorraine Moller said, 'For me, running is a lifestyle and an art. I'm far more interested in the magic of it than the mechanics.' There will be runners who are happy to do their own thing and those that would benefit from other runners around them. The key is to find the magic, no matter how you get there (as long as it's not on a bike).

THESE GIRLS CAN

••

❝ There's not a better feeling than when you have found that moment of balance and harmony when both running and life come together. Then you know why you run and that you couldn't live without it. ❞

JOAN BENOIT, ATHLETE

CITIUS, ALTIUS, FORTIUS

Female runners, revved up and ready to compete with their male counterparts, are now commonplace in any non-single-sex road race. There are specific women-only races – the most notable in the UK being the Cancer Research Race for Life series – but the overwhelming majority pit Jill against John and let the best athlete win. Nowadays on the track, women line up against like-minded female competitors in the same race distances as men. But this hasn't always been the case.

In 1892 when Baron Pierre de Coubertin announced that he intended to revive the ancient Olympic Games, he could not have foreseen the manner in which the movement would grow in the years that followed the inaugural modern Games in 1896. The

International Olympic Committee (IOC) was created in June 1894 under the banner of the Olympic Movement, which now also includes the organising committees of the Olympic Games and International Federations. The Olympic Charter codifies the fundamental principles of Olympism into seven statements, one of which states thus: 'The practice of sport is a human right. Every individual must have the possibility of practising sport, without discrimination of any kind and in the Olympic spirit, which requires mutual understanding with a spirit of friendship, solidarity and fair play.'

The Movement hasn't always been entirely fair in its treatment of female athletes despite its stated aims. As mentioned on p.12, in the early ancient Olympiads only men were allowed to compete, and married women were not even allowed to watch. When the modern Olympics were recreated in 1886 no female took part in the Games, although it was reported at the time that at least one female protestor, Stamata Revithi, ran the marathon route the day after Spyridon Louis won the race. A second woman may also have run, but the records are not clear. In the eyes of the men who ran the sport, the role of women was to be admired, and their athletic ability was limited. Even the medal from the II Olympiad in 1900 illustrates this belief, depicting as it did a winged goddess, arms aloft holding laurel branches. On the back, the engraving depicts a male athlete in a similar pose.

'Give a girl the right shoes and she can conquer the world,' said Marilyn Monroe years later. Marilyn was right, but, always ahead of her time, the world would have to wait a few years for the IOC and the International Association of Athletic Federations (IAAF) to catch up with her.

The first year that athletes took an Olympic oath, which was read during the opening ceremony, was in 1920. The original oath, read by Victor Boin, was: 'We swear that we will take part in the Olympic Games in a spirit of chivalry, for the honour of our country and for the glory of sport.' The oath was read at every summer Games by a man until 1972 when Heidi Schüller became the first woman to do so. She was only just behind Mexican athlete Norma Enriqueta Basilio de Sotelo who made history in 1968 as the first woman athlete to light the Olympic cauldron at the Games.

It would be many years, however, before there would be anything remotely approaching equality in terms of athletic endeavour. Women were not allowed to compete in an athletic event until the 1928 Games in Amsterdam with the longest race being 800 m. One woman briefly collapsed at the end of the race, and that was enough for the IOC to ban women competing at the event until 1960. Amsterdam also saw the first 100 m women's contest, which American Betty Robinson won in what was then a record time of 12.02. Betty was clearly a whippet, helping the USA to a silver medal in the 4 x 100 m relay. Following a horrific car crash in 1931 that threatened her ability to even walk, she returned to claim her second gold medal in the 4 x 100 m relay in the 1936 Games but not in the individual event. It was not until 1968 that a woman would win back-to-back gold medals in successive 100 m finals, when 23-year-old Wyomia Tyus claimed her second medal in a new world record in the Mexico Games.

The IAAF did not recognise world records in the 1,500 m for women until 1967, records in the 3,000 m until 1972 and records in the 5,000 m and 10,000 m until 1981. The IAAF were slightly ahead of the Olympic Movement, but not by far. In 1972 women were finally permitted to run 1,500 m at the Olympics when Lyudmila Bragina won gold. In 1988 women were allowed to compete in an Olympic 10,000 m and 1996 in the 5,000 m. The lack of events in the Olympic Games for female athletes to compete in so many years after the inaugural modern games began, highlights how the IOC failed to achieve equality until relatively recently and not just in the early years of the movement.

HISTORY OF EVENTS AND ENTRANTS IN THE MODERN OLYMPICS

Year	Venue	Number of athletes	Number of men	Number of women	Number of events	Number of sports/ disciplines
1886	Athens	241	241	0	43	9
1900	Paris	997	975	22	95	18
1904	St Louis	651	645	6	91	17
1908	London	2,008	1,971	37	110	22
1912	Stockholm	2,407	2,359	48	102	14
1920	Antwerp	2,626	2,561	65	154	22
1924	Paris	3,089	2,954	135	126	17
1928	Amsterdam	2,883	2,606	277	109	14
1932	Los Angeles	1,332	1,206	126	117	14
1936	Berlin	3,963	3,632	331	129	19
1948	London	4,104	3,714	390	136	17
1952	Helsinki	4,955	4,436	519	149	17
1956	Melbourne/ Stockholm	3,314	2,938	376	145	17

1960	Rome	5,338	4,727	611	150	17
1964	Tokyo	5,151	4,473	678	163	19
1968	Mexico	5,516	4,735	781	172	23
1972	Munich	7,134	6,075	1,059	195	23
1976	Montreal	6,084	4,824	1,260	198	21
1980	Moscow	5,179	4,064	1,115	203	21
1984	Los Angeles	6,829	5,263	1,566	221	23
1988	Seoul	8,391	6,197	2,194	237	25
1992	Barcelona	9,356	6,652	2,704	257	28
1996	Atlanta	10,318	6,806	3,512	271	26
2000	Sydney	10,651	6,582	4,069	300	28
2004	Athens	10,625	6,296	4,329	301	28
2008	Beijing	10,942	6,305	4,637	302	28
2012	London	10,567	5,892	4,675	302	26
2016	Rio de Janeiro	11,200*			306	42

*At the time of writing The Olympic Studies Centre were unable to confirm the exact number of athletes in the 2016 Games and this is a provisional figure. They estimated that of the total number of athletes approximately 44.8 per cent were women.

A cursory glance at the table above shows how long it has taken the Olympic Movement to consign gender based discrimination to history in terms of the number of athletes taking part in the Games across the full sporting spectrum. At the 2012 Games in London, Brunei, Qatar and Saudi Arabia sent women athletes to participate. For the first time in the Games' history dating – back to 776 BC – every country that was eligible to compete had sent a female athlete and, following the introduction of women's boxing, women competed at every sport.

NINETEEN EIGHTY-FOUR

George Orwell's dystopian literary masterpiece created a disturbing vision of society, where omnipresent government surveillance persecuted individuals who did not adopt Big Brother's party line. The Orwellian attitude of the IOC to women competing in distance events was, in that year, subject to a paradigm shift in thinking, when the first female Olympic marathon took place. The 1984 race featured well-established and renowned road running athletes including Joan Benoit, Grete Waitz, Ingrid Kristiansen and Rosa Mota. Benoit won in 2:24:52 and said after the event, 'I thought about the work and sacrifice of countless women and men who had made my opportunity to run the Olympic Marathon possible. I was very conscious I was part of history.' And indeed she was.

THE ROAD RUNNING FRATERNITY

In road running terms, the Olympic Movement lagged behind their brethren on the tarmac circuit, but not by far. One of the oldest races on the US circuit, The Turkey Trot, would not allow women to compete until 1972 when Mary Ann Bolles placed one hundred and forty-second out of 169 finishers. How times have changed, along with the women's record. In 2016, it was held by Victoria Mitchell in 26:21, who clearly loved the race as she won it eight times between 1991 and 2000.

Another US event that began near the turn of the twentieth century – The Dipsea Race – denied women the right to enter officially until 1971, although unofficially they had been in the race since 1950. The organisers of the Dipsea Race did put on all women's races between 1918 and 1922 when they had more entrants than the men's equivalent.

The oldest marathon, Boston, finally opened its doors to women in 1972, five years after Kathrine Switzer's glass-ceiling-shattering run at the event. The first official female winner of the 1972 event was Nina Kuscsik. But, while Switzer was the first woman to have run the course with a bib (mistakenly given to her by the race organisers who mistook her for a man) she wasn't the first woman to ever have run the Boston course: Roberta Gibb ran it three times without an official number.

The New York marathon began in 1970 and a year later allowed women to run. The first race was won by 19-year-old Beth Bonner in a time of 2:55:22, with only five other women in the event. In 1972, that rose to six, and in 1973 to 12. By 1980 female participants were still only at the 1,962 mark in comparison to the 12,050 men who took part in the race. The number of women who are now competing in New York is not that far off the men.

By 1974 Switzer lead the charge for open-minded, supportive athletes of both genders when she won the New York event in 3:07:29, and she continues to blaze the trail today. When Switzer ran Boston she did so under the number 261, which became the inspiration for the 261 Fearless Movement and 261 Women's Marathon held in Palma, Majorca. This is a women-only event and, while there are a number of others around the world, races at that distance for women alone are not common.

When the London Marathon began in 1981 there was a similar divide between the sexes for a number of years, but it has evolved in the same way as the New York Marathon with regard to female participation, and the disparity between genders is gradually narrowing. Joyce Smith won the inaugural women's race and came back a year later at the age of 44 to reclaim her crown. Smith was an ordinary mother and housewife who would drop her children at school, go off and train, collect them and juggle all sorts of demands without athletic funding, sports agents, a team of physiotherapists, or access to world-class training facilities. Smith originally began her career in shorter distances, reaching the semi-finals of the 1500 m at the 1972 Olympics before stepping up to run a women-only marathon in Tokyo in 1979 with 53 other competitors. She won that race, returned and repeated the feat in 1980 before turning her attention to London.

Notably, the turning point in women's distance running was in 1984 with the first women's Olympic marathon. The top nine women broke the 2:30 barrier, and this was a time that had only been achieved by two women prior to the Olympic race. But not every woman who took part in that first Olympic marathon finished well. Gabriela Andersen-Schiess approached the finish line 20 minutes after Benoit had won, exhausted, dehydrated and struggling to stand. Race officials came rushing over to help her but, unlike Dorando Pietri, 76 years before her, Gabriela waved away any offer of assistance. Had she been helped she would have been out of the race and she knew it. It took her almost six minutes to cover the final 400 m before crossing the line and collapsing.

In 1928, the IOC had used the excuse of one woman collapsing over the line in the 800 m to suspend their involvement in that event. This time, the watching public were enthralled by the drama unfolding in front of them. Rather than see a woman who could not cope with the distance, they witnessed an athlete's determination to finish.

In the 1984 Olympic Games, 1,566 women competed, which was a record at the time. Every four years since the numbers have steadily increased, to the point that they are approaching equality with men. In 1984 roughly a quarter of the medals were awarded to women; by 2016 this had risen to almost 45 per cent in the Rio Olympics. It would not be an overstatement to say that the first women's Olympic marathon race inspired a generation of women to pull on their trainers and join male runners on the track, the streets or on the trails, believing that they too were capable of achieving the impossible.

FASCINATING FACT

The 1984 Games saw Moroccan Nawal El Moutawakel win the inaugural women's 400 m hurdles gold medal, creating a host of personal firsts in the process. Olga Bondarenko of the Soviet Union won the first women's 10,000 m gold medal in Seoul 1988, and China's Wang Junxia won the first women's 5,000 m gold medal in Atlanta 1996.

Three decades later and the road running scene around the world would seem a very strange place if men only toed the start line. Athletes are athletes regardless of their age, sex, origin, religion or any other external factor. Looking back at it from today's viewpoint, it is very difficult to understand how such discrimination was ever allowed.

There are women-only events all around the world that attract thousands of athletes. For example, The Hans Christian Anderson Half and Full Marathon takes place in Denmark, the RunGirl 13.1 in the US and I Can Half Marathon in India. At the other end of the scale, shorter events continue to attract large numbers, including The Great Women's 10 k or obstacle races such as the Mudderella. Many are serious races for committed athletes, but not all are. Those wanting to combine a bit of exercise and fun need look no further than the Race for Life series. Where else can you join 1,000 other women walking or running through the streets in fancy dress, wearing underwear as outerwear, having a ball and aiding advances in medical science in the process? If anything, men are being left behind in this new running revolution given that the Y-front 5 k series is yet to take hold.

INSPIRATIONAL RUNNERS

···

❝ We can't all be heroes because somebody has to sit on the curb and clap as they go by. ❞

WILL ROGERS, US HUMORIST

JAMES 'JESSE' CLEVELAND OWENS (1913–1980)

NICKNAME: THE BUCKEYE BULLET

❝ Find the good. It's all around you. Find it, showcase it and you'll start believing it. ❞

JESSE OWENS, ATHLETE

Born in Oakville, Alabama, during the First World War, Owens was an African-American who took part in a race widely regarded as the greatest of all time, winning gold in the 100 m final at the Berlin Olympics on 3 August 1936. That medal, along with three further golds won in the 200 m, the long jump and the 100 m relay in the same Games, remains an evocative symbol of one man's triumph over the fascism of Nazi Germany and its abhorrent racial ideals of an Aryan super race that 'would last for 1,000 years'. The summer Games were designed to promote the ideals of Nazism and give Hitler's rhetoric and the Third Reich's propaganda a world platform. Guy Walters records in *Berlin Games: How Hitler Stole the Olympic Dream* that the Führer's Minister of Propaganda, Joseph Goebbels, wrote in his diary that 'white humanity should be ashamed of itself', after three African-Americans won gold medals during one day of the Games. Despite their achievements, it is Owens who was the star of the show with his gold medal haul.

The political significance of Owens' wins, and those of his contemporaries, such as Cornelius Johnson in the high jump, shouldn't overshadow the track achievements of an athlete who has been described as 'perfection personified'. Prior to the Games, he broke world records for the long jump, low hurdles and various sprint distances. In Berlin he ran 10.3 seconds in the first round of the 100 m, 10.2 in the second round for new world and Olympic records (subsequently disallowed due to the tail wind), 10.4 in the semi-final and 10.3 in the final, when the wind was also too strong. The German Erich Borchmeyer (who Owens had beaten in a 100-yard race in Los Angeles Memorial Coliseum in 1932) trailed in second from last.

On 4 August, he set a new Games record of 21.1 in the 200 m heats and bettered that in the final with 20.7. He didn't dominate the long jump, almost going out in the first round, but eventually beat another German into second place with leaps of 7.94 m and 8.06 m. On 8 August, he helped the relay team to a new world record in the 4 x 100 m. His achievements would not be repeated until Carl Lewis' performance in the 1984 Olympics in Los Angeles.

Owens left a lasting legacy that continues to inspire beyond the confines of sporting success.

GRETE WAITZ
(1953–2011)

NICKNAME: GRANDMA

" When I came to New York in 1978, I was a full-time school teacher and track runner, and determined to retire from competitive running. But winning the New York City Marathon kept me running for another decade. "
GRETE WAITZ, ATHLETE

Winning the New York City Marathon certainly changed Norwegian Grete Waitz from a good track runner into the world's best female marathon runner of her era. In her youth, Waitz set European junior records, although her senior career was mixed with significant success and failure on the track, as she failed to make two Olympic finals in the 1970s. In 1978, she was invited to run by New York City Marathon race director and founder, Fred Lebow. Almost by accident, she found her most successful race distance. On her marathon debut, she ran a world record time of 2:32:29, reducing it in 1979 to 2:27:33 and to 2:25:41 in 1980. She would eventually win the race nine times, lowering the world record in London in 1983 to 2:25:29 and winning gold at the Helsinki World Championships that year. In 1984 she won silver at the inaugural women's Olympic marathon. She won London again in 1986 and Stockholm in 1988, but was forced to retire from the 1988 Games with a knee injury. In 1992, she ran New York City with the terminally ill Lebow, who passed away two years later.

She also won many shorter road and cross-country events, including the famous Falmouth Road Race. She decimated the course record at the Great North Run in 1984 with a time of 1:10:27 and she also medalled at the World Cross Country Championships seven times. At a time when marathon running for the masses was growing, Waitz's achievements led the way for women to enter races of that length, building on the inspiration of Bobbi Gibb who, without a race number, unofficially finished the Boston Marathon in 1966 and Kathrine Switzer, the first official female finisher, a year later. Waitz transcended gender stereotypes and will forever remain an icon to male and female runners alike.

STEVE ROLAND PREFONTAINE
(1951–1975)

NICKNAME: PRE

*❝ A lot of people run a race to see who is fastest.
I run to see who has the most guts. ❞*

STEVE PREFONTAINE, ATHLETE

Born in Coos Bay, Oregon, 'Pre' was a cross-country and track school and college runner who rose to international stardom before his death in a car crash at the age of just 24, setting a host of records at distances ranging between 2,000–10,000 m. Whilst at the University of Oregon he won multiple NCAA (National Collegiate Athletic Association) titles, setting nine collegiate track records in the process. In 1970, he made the cover of *Sports Illustrated* and in 1972, at the age of 21, he finished fourth in the Olympic 5,000 m in a time of 13:28.4, behind Lasse Virén (13:26.4), Mohammed Gammoudi (13:27.4) and Ian Stewart (13:27.6). He brought athletics to a wider audience in America along with runners including Frank Shorter, who arguably were the catalyst for the running boom of the 1970s. At the time of his death, Pre held every American record between 2,000 and 10,000 m.

PREFONTAINE'S RECORDS

- 2,000 m – 5:01.4, 9 May 1975

- 3,000 m – 7:42.6, 2 July 1974

- 5,000 m – 13:21.87, 26 June 1974

- 10,000 m – 27:43.8, 27 April 1974

- 2 miles (3.2 km) – 8:18.29, 18 July 1974

- 3 miles (4.8 km) – 12:51.4, 8 June 1974

- 6 miles (9.6 km) – 26:51.8, 27 April 1974

The loss of such a talent sent shockwaves around the world and yet Prefontaine's legacy lives on. At the rock where his life ended, a memorial reads, 'For your dedication and loyalty, To your principles and beliefs... For your love, warmth, and friendship. For your family and friends... You are missed by so many and you will never be forgotten...' And he's not. Since 1975, an international track event called the Prefontaine Classic has been held in Eugene, Oregon, and the 10 k Prefontaine Memorial Run takes place each September in Coos Bay. For a runner there can be no better tribute than a race being held in your honour.

KATHRINE SWITZER
(1947–PRESENT)

NICKNAME: THE MARATHON WOMAN

*66 When I go to the Boston Marathon now, I have
wet shoulders – women fall into my arms crying.
They're weeping for joy because running has changed
their lives. They feel they can do anything. 99*

KATHRINE SWITZER, RUNNER AND AUTHOR

The first Boston marathon took place in 1897, with just 15
male runners. It was a bastion of prejudice and women were
not allowed to enter. In 1967, using just her initials, Kathrine
Switzer was able to secure a number and ran with her coach
Arnie Briggs and boyfriend, Tom Miller. Four miles into the
race, an official, Jock Semple, lunged and tried to snatch her
number screaming 'get the hell out of my race' in full view
of the watching media truck which had been following from
early in the race. A swift shove from Miller sent him flying and
changed the course of athletics history. Eventually finishing in
approximately 4:20, the event transformed her into a prominent
figurehead in the fight to allow women to compete in long-
distance races.

Switzer became a champion of the right for women to enter
races and campaigned tirelessly for an Olympic women's
marathon. In 1972, Boston finally opened its doors to all. In
Athletic terms, Switzer was an accomplished runner, winning
the New York City Marathon in 3:07:29 in 1973 (with times

of 3:16:02 and 3:02:57 in the straddling years) and with a personal best of 2:51:37 at the Boston Marathon in 1975, which most marathon runners would give their teeth for. She was named Female Runner of the Decade (1967–77) by *Runner's World*, became an author, and continues to inspire men and women alike.

CHRIS BRASHER (1928–2003) AND JOHN DISLEY (1928–2016)

INTERESTING FACT: BRASHER FOUNDED CHRIS BRASHER'S SPORTING EMPORIUM WHICH WOULD LATER BECOME SWEATSHOP

> ❝ *The human race can be one joyous family, working together, laughing together, achieving the impossible.* ❞
>
> **CHRIS BRASHER, ATHLETE**

Brasher was many things, including a journalist, and he wrote the quote above in *The Observer* in 1979 about the New York Marathon. Having witnessed what New York brought to its streets he wanted the same experience in London. He was also a runner with an extraordinary pedigree. Along with Chris Chataway, he paced Roger Bannister to the first sub-four-minute mile in 1954. He won the Olympic 3,000 m steeplechase in 1956 and created the Sweatshop Running chain. Brasher was no slouch at the longer distances, finishing the 1979 New York marathon in an age-graded time of 2:58:53.

He would later become the President of the Association of International Marathons and Distance Races, and the recipient of a CBE in 1996. He was survived by John Disley who was also an international athlete of some acclaim. Disley was a former world record holder in the 3,000 m steeplechase, Britain's first world-class steeplechaser and Olympic bronze medallist. He lowered the British steeplechase record an impressive five times from 9:18.4 in 1950 to 8:44.2 by 1955. He took part in the Melbourne Olympics in 1956, placing sixth in the final won by Brasher. The two men would later be highly influential in raising the profile of orienteering in Britain, and Disley took over from Brasher as Chairman of the British Orienteering Federation in the 1970s. His knowledge and experience in course distance verification led to the creation of *The Measurement of Road Race Courses* manual.

Brasher and Disley were also the driving forces behind the London Marathon, which was famously created over a pint or two in the Dysart Arms. The 1981 London Marathon saw Dick Beardsley and Inge Simonsen crossing the line together in a dead heat in 2:11:48, followed not long after by Joyce Smith with a British record of 2:29:57. The two men remained lifelong friends and despite their own personal and individual achievements, it is perhaps their combined foresight and imagination through the creation of the 1981 London race that will leave the biggest imprint on the memory of the million plus runners who have now covered the course.

JOANNE MARIE 'JO' PAVEY
(1973-PRESENT)

INTERESTING FACT: JO ALWAYS WEARS LONG WHITE SOCKS THAT STOP JUST BELOW HER KNEE WHEN RACING

❝ It feels a bit surreal. It is really special to think I am 40 with two children. ❞

JO PAVEY, ATHLETE (AFTER WINNING 10,000 M GOLD AT THE EUROPEAN CHAMPIONSHIPS)

Pavey is a British-born elite runner who, in 2016, at the age of 42, having given birth to two children, made it to her fifth Olympic Games in Rio de Janeiro, finishing fifth in the 10,000 m final. She has experienced many highs and equally as many lows in her professional career, having been blighted a number of times by injury and illness. It's not just her longevity that makes Pavey an inspiring athlete, but also the way she has dealt with difficulties that might have made other athletes hang up their spikes years ago.

As a youngster, she was a precious talent winning the English Schools' Athletic Association 1,500 m title and setting a British U15's record of 4:27:9 in 1998 (eight places and 13 seconds behind her was a certain Paula Radcliffe). Pavey would eventually go on to record a personal best at that distance of 4:01:79 in Monaco in 2003, but would also set records at many other distances. While still an amateur, Pavey won a number of Amateur Athletic Association titles and made her senior debut in 1997. She ran events covering many distances from the 1,500 m up to the marathon which she ran in London in 2011 in a time of 2:28:24.

However, on many occasions when she was in contention for a medal at a major world championship, bad luck stopped her from fulfilling her true potential. On the eve of the 2002 Commonwealth Games she developed a bacterial infection which hampered preparation. At the 2005 European Indoor Championships a calf injury forced her to drop out of the race. Before the 2007 European Indoor Championships in Birmingham she was badly affected by a heavy bout of flu, which led to her finishing in sixth place in the 3,000 m with a time of 8:54.94. Just a few months later, in a race in London and fully fit, Jo ran 8:44.13 which would have given her second place in the earlier European race. Over her career she has suffered multiple stress fractures, meaning that she's been forced to take long breaks to recuperate. Then, in the lead-up to the 2016 Olympics, she developed a chest infection and virus that led to her scraping into the British team almost at the last possible moment.

At national level, Pavey secured many titles including 5,000 m on six different occasions. At international level she took part in championships around the world, often just finishing outside the medal table, but she never gave up. At the Commonwealth Games, World Cups, World Athletics finals, European Cross Country Championships, Continental Cup and European Championships she has secured five bronze medals, two silver medals and two gold medals in competitions stretching from 2002 to 2014. Her first gold was in 2006, but for many avid fans it was her 2014 gold in the European Championships in Switzerland that was her crowning glory.

A little more than a month before turning 41, she became the oldest female to win gold in the history of the Championships when she secured the 10,000 m title. The Exeter AC member even wore a vest on that night that was older than a number of the runners she was competing against. Dame Kelly Holmes wrote after that race, 'I'm not someone who cries, but I cried watching her race,' and said she had never seen her race so well. A few days after that same race, she was able to secure a bronze medal in the 5,000 m. Pavey's philosophy is simple, 'I don't get stressed about my running. I don't dwell on it. I just do it.'

EMIL ZÁTOPEK
(1922–2000)

NICKNAME: THE LOCOMOTIVE

> ❝ When a person trains once, nothing happens. When a person forces himself to do a thing a hundred or a thousand times, then he certainly has developed in more ways than physical. Is it raining? That doesn't matter. Am I tired? That doesn't matter, either. Then willpower will be no problem. ❞
>
> **EMIL ZÁTOPEK, ATHLETE**

Zátopek was a Czech legend who won five Olympic medals, broke 18 world records and was undefeated at 10,000 m for a full six years. Between September 1948 and June 1951, he ran 75 races in distances ranging from 3,000–10,000 m and won them all. That is still the longest ever running win streak. He achieved three gold medals at the Helsinki Olympics, including in his debut marathon, a feat that is unlikely ever to be repeated.

Despite being known for his high volume, intensive interval training, he wasn't the inventor of it, but he did take it to a level that had never previously been reached. He had an almost unparalleled ability to withstand pain and put his body through training so rigorous that, in the early days, it was derided by the so-called experts around him. As the great man himself said, 'It's at the borders of pain and suffering that the men are separated from the boys.'

Even now, a cursory glance at Zátopek's training manual would leave many an athlete bandaging their jaw. He would take part in sessions on a daily basis that would include 100 laps of a 400 m track at a fast pace, with jog recoveries in between each effort. His training was simply ferocious and to this day his methods influence elite runners and amateurs alike, albeit on varying scales.

It is estimated that he ran over 50,000 miles in his lifetime, most of which would have been at a very high quality. He wasn't prolific in shorter distances, with lifetime bests of 1:58.7 in the 800 m and 3:52.8 in the 1,500 m which, while good, are not extraordinary in elite terms. He was a mid- and long-distance maestro. In one race alone in Houstka Spa on 26 October 1952, he set world records for 15 miles (1:16:24.8), 25 k (1:19:11.8) and 30 k (1:35:23.8). He didn't run with a particularly smooth motion and there are many photographs of him head bent to one side, his face contorted in pain. As he pointed out, 'I shall learn to have a better style once they start judging races according to their beauty.'

For distance runners in particular, he remains inspirational to this day. He motivated those around him as evidenced by the words of Ron Clarke, a world-class athlete who secured 17 world records in his career, when he said, 'There is not and never was, a greater man than Emil Zátopek.' It is likely that Zátopek would have preferred that description over his biographer's, Richard Asquith, who said, 'Like any serious runner, he was a bit of a nutter.' Both have a point and, actually, he probably would have agreed that both descriptions were accurate.

PAULA JANE RADCLIFFE
(1973–PRESENT)

NICKNAME: QUEEN PAULA

It's important that athletes can compete on a level playing field. And youngsters coming into the sport can know that if they are working hard and training hard, they'll see a true reflection of where they stand and what they can achieve worldwide and not be swayed by people who are cheating.
PAULA RADCLIFFE, ATHLETE

The Bedford and County athlete is, to many athletic fans, not just the best British long-distance runner but the greatest there has ever been. She has won a staggering number of titles since joining her club at the age of 11. By the time she was 16, she was competing in the Junior World Cross Country Championships when she came fifteenth and established herself as an emerging athlete. By 1992 she had secured gold in the World Cross Country Championships in the under 20s race in a time of 13:30, having already won a host of medals on the domestic cross-country scene at both Inter-Counties and English National levels. In the following years, her successes grew, securing the top spot at the British World Cross Country, UK and Amateur Athletics Association championships.

At senior level, Paula moved onto the track where her career faltered and she was, for a number of years, the nearly girl of British athletics. As a spectator and fan, it was a difficult period and it must have been a great deal worse for Paula herself. In far too many races, she would lead for long periods only to be overtaken in the final straight and pushed out of the medals. At 3,000 m she came fourth three times in major finals. At 5,000 m she secured one bronze, as well as two fourth and two fifth place finishes. The agonising fourth place appeared again in two major finals at 10,000 m along with a silver in the seventh IAAF World Championship's in 1999. Her personal best for 3,000 m of 8:22.20 (Commonwealth Record) and 5,000 m of 14:29.11 (National Record) were just not quite good enough on the world stage. At European level she did secure six first place finishes in the 3,000 m, 5,000 m and 10,000 m races.

She continued to compete in cross country, notably winning the Senior Women's Race at the World Cross Country Championships in 2001 and 2002, but it was in road-based events that she really made her mark. In 2003, Paula secured a World Best at 10 k of 30:21 which still stands. She won the World Half Marathon Championships between 2000 and 2003, securing a World Best of 1:05:40 and National Record of 1:06:47 in the process. She won London Marathon in 2002, 2003 and 2005, Chicago Marathon in 2003, New York Marathon in 2004 and 2007 and the World Championships marathon in 2005. Her 2003 London win in a World Best time of 2:15:25 is arguably the greatest piece of distance running ever, and it's a time that hasn't been challenged since. In the IAAF rankings Paula holds the three best times ever and four in the top ten. Although there has been disappointment particularly at the Olympics caused by factors beyond her control, the sheer number of national and international successes still places her in a class of her own.

Her vociferous opposition to drug cheats lasted throughout her career. At the 2001 World Championships she memorably held a banner that read 'EPO Cheats Out' after Russian athlete Olga Yegorova was allowed to compete after failing a drug test. She continues to be an ardent supporter of the World Anti-Doping Agency, promotes sport at grassroots level and will be an inspiration to athletes of all abilities for many years to come.

THOMAS (TOMMIE) C. SMITH
(1944-PRESENT)
AND JOHN CARLOS
(1945-PRESENT)

NICKNAME: TOMMIE THE JET

> " *If I win I am American, not a black American. But if I did something bad, then they would say 'a negro'. We are black and we are proud of being black.* "
>
> **TOMMIE SMITH, ATHLETE**

The 1968 Olympics were held in Mexico and the 200 m men's final on 16 October was won by the USA's Tommie Smith. Second place was taken by Australia's Peter Norman and the bronze was won by American John Carlos. Against a background of segregation in America, civil unrest and the assassinations of Robert Kennedy and Dr Martin Luther King, Smith and Carlos wanted to make a political statement. They walked to the medal podium without shoes, wearing one black glove each. When the National Anthem was played, they raised their gloved fists in a Black Power salute and bowed their heads. The two Americans had also prepared other symbols: Smith's black scarf represented black pride, and Carlos wore beads for black people who 'were lynched, or killed, that no one said a prayer for, that were hung and tarred. It was for those thrown off the side of the boats in the middle passage'. Not wearing shoes represented black poverty.

There was an outcry over this political demonstration, with the IOC calling the silent protest 'a deliberate and violent breach of the fundamental principles of the Olympic spirit'. *Time* magazine called it a 'public display of petulance'. At the moment of their greatest sporting triumph, the two athletes choose to put the needs of others before their own and draw attention to the plight of others in a way that they hoped would lead to lasting change. Looking back from what are hopefully more enlightened times, it is difficult to comprehend for those who did not witness first-hand the impact this gesture had in the USA and around the world. It helped to bring focus on inequality, prejudice and the civil rights movement. The symbolism of the act transcends the years and is a powerful reminder of what sport can achieve.

THE SUB-FOUR-MINUTE MILE

> ❝ *Whether we athletes liked it or not, the four-minute mile had become rather like an Everest; a challenge to the human spirit, it was a barrier that seemed to defy all attempts to break it, an irksome reminder that men's striving might be in vain.* ❞
>
> **ROGER BANNISTER, ATHLETE**

THE HISTORY

Attempts to run a mile in a time faster than four minutes captured the public's imagination long before the feat was finally achieved on 6 May 1954 at Iffley Road, Oxford, by Roger Bannister in a time of 3:59.40. By the 1700s in Britain and further afield, gambling on races of differing distances, including the mile, was widespread, with reports appearing in publications such as *The Sporting Magazine* of large wagers being placed. One of the first athletics books, *Pedestrianism*, recounts an attempt at the start of the nineteenth century to run a measured street mile – and whilst the reported time of 4:10 is impressive, it is impossible to confirm. With the sums involved and the incentives to manipulate these events, reliance can't be placed on the accuracy of records of the day.

FASCINATING FACT

The 'metric mile' in race terms is the 1,500 m and is commonly run by professional athletes on a track. It is 19 yards 21 inches short of a Roman mile, which was 1,000 Roman strides (a stride being two paces).

THE PROS vs AMATEURS

The growth of professional promoters and runners aided the cause of breaking the four-minute mile barrier, as it led to athletes with training regimes whose sole purpose was to make money, and to races taking place on enclosed tracks, which the public had to pay to enter. These could be more accurately measured and timed, using systems that had been developed for horse racing. Ironically, in the years that followed the creation of the AAA, the conflict between professionals and amateurs hindered the four-minute barrier being broken.

The organisation imposed a strict code seeking to ensure that the custodians of the sport as they saw it – the gentleman amateurs who ran for pleasure rather than financial gain – were the only ones whose records counted. The amateurs were, by their nature, part-time athletes who did not train to the standard needed to break the barrier.

A verifiable benchmark of 4:12.75 was set in an accurate, timed race by professional Walter George in 1886, a record which stood for 29 years until it was edged by Norman Taber in 1915 with 4:12.6. George's time was not recognised by the amateur authorities, who still hold American John Paul Jones' time of 4:14.4 set in 1913 as the first world record.

It is difficult to pinpoint the moment the potential for breaking the barrier became a realistic objective. Did runners at the turn of the nineteenth century truly believe it would happen? Certainly many coaches of the era didn't, and the longer George's record stood, the further away the prospect seemed.

The modern comparison is the sub-two-hour marathon barrier. It seems such an impossible task and yet, since Spyridon Louis' marathon time of 2:58:50 in the 1896 Olympics, the world record has dropped by nearly 56 minutes to 2:02:57. Will future generations wonder why it took so long to be broken? It is the sense of anticipation that makes the sub-two-hour potential as exciting as the sub-four-minute mile was in the 1950s.

A MATTER OF TIME

In the years that followed George and Taber, runners including Paavo Nurmi in the 1920s and Jack Lovelock in the 1930s reduced the world record. Glenn Cunningham ran the mile in 4:04.4 on an indoor, wind-free track, which was therefore not recognised as a record. Nevertheless, it suggested that the barrier could be broken.

By the 1940s, Gunder Hägg and Arne Andersson had equalled or lowered the record six times, with the former recording 4:01.4

in 1945. It had taken 59 years to shave just over 11 seconds off George's time. It was so close, and the sense of excitement at the prospect of breaking the barrier touched athletes and the public all over the globe thanks to increasingly sophisticated means of communication. The eight years and 293 days following Hägg's record were one of the most exciting periods in the mile's history, as runners such as Bannister, Wes Santee and John Landy tried to break the barrier time and time again.

MILE BENCHMARK TIMES BEFORE BANNISTER

1886 Walter George 4:12.75
1913 John Paul Jones 4:14.4 – IAAF first world record
1915 Norman Taber 4:12.6
1923 Paavo Nurmi 4:10.4
1931 Jules Ladoumègue 4:09.2
1933 Jack Lovelock 4:07.6
1934 Glenn Cunningham 4:06.8
1937 Sydney Wooderson 4:06.4
1942 Gunder Hägg 4:06.2
1942 Arne Andersson 4:06.2
1942 Gunder Hägg 4:04.6
1943 Arne Andersson 4:02.6
1944 Arne Andersson 4:01.6
1945 Gunder Hägg 4:01.4

THE RACE

Bannister was an Oxford medical student and part-time athlete, who adopted a professional approach to the mile attempt following his failure to win a medal at the previous Olympic Games. Pacers were strictly not allowed in the 1950s, which is why his running-mates on the day, Chris Chataway and Chris Brasher, had to be seen to be trying to run the race as well as they could. The reality is that the three friends had trained meticulously together working out the pace needed for each lap. The race was broadcast live on BBC radio and commentated by the 1924 Olympic medallist Harold Abrahams. The organised and rehearsed race plan came together as they hit each lap target, until Bannister crossed the line and ran into the history books. 'In the last 50 yards my body had long since exhausted its energy but it went on running just the same,' said Bannister, who admitted that it was Chataway and Brasher who got him there.

OH SO CLOSE

Wes Santee ran 4:01.4 just 23 days after Bannister's record, equalling Hägg's 1945 world record; shortly afterwards in another race he recorded a time of 4:00.6. On 21 June 1954, John Landy became 'the Buzz Aldrin and Sherpa Tenzing of the athletics world', recording a mile time in 3:57.9 (rounded up to 3:58), shattering Bannister's record that had lasted a mere 46 days.

FASCINATING FACT

In the 'Race of the Century' at the British Empire and Commonwealth Games in Vancouver, British Columbia, on 7 August 1954, Bannister and Landy became the first men in history to record a time lower than four minutes in the same race; Bannister edged it in 3:58.8 with Landy finishing in 3:59.6.

By 1957, Herb Elliott reduced the record to 3:54.5 and in the years that followed the record fell still further, although the 3:50 barrier resisted strongly. It wasn't until 1975 that John Walker, of New Zealand, ran 3:49.4. The current list of the ten fastest mile times ever run is dominated by Morocco's Hicham El Guerrouj, who appears an astonishing seven times. His 1999 world record benchmark of 3:43.13 stands supreme.

WHY IS IT SPECIAL?

Bannister's run has stood the test of time as one of the landmark achievements in history, and not just in athletics. After the barrier had been broken, he compared it with climbing Everest for the first time. The first person to climb Everest? Hillary. First on the moon? Armstrong. First to run a four-minute mile? Actually, it was Derek Ibbotson, who ran an exact 240 seconds on 3 September 1957. Due to a nanosecond, however, it's the now-famous medical student's achievement that will forever be linked with the mile.

FASCINATING FACT

The fastest one-mile sack race is 16:41, set on 19 May 2007 by Ashrita Furman (USA) in Baruun Salaa in Mongolia.

Anyone who has ever attempted to run a fast mile knows one thing – it hurts. A miler has to have the perfect combination of strength, speed and endurance. For the sprinters it's over all too quickly. For the 5,000 m or longer, races are run at a patient, planned pace, with breaks for the line in the latter stages. The mile requires intense effort from the gun, with each compelling lap tightening the grip on the observer. 'Almost every part of the mile is tactically important; you can never let down, never stop thinking and you can be beaten at almost any point. I suppose you could say it's like life,' said Landy. The pain is etched in the faces of athletes on the home straight. Knowing they have pushed their bodies to near total physical exertion, and their minds to their threshold, is inspirational.

WORLD TRACK RECORDS FOR THE MILE – WOMEN

Time	Name	Nationality	Race location	Date
4:17.44	Maricica Puică	Romania	Rieti	16 Sept 1982
4:17.33	Maricica Puică	Romania	Zürich	21 Aug 1985

4:17.25	Sonia O'Sullivan	Ireland	Oslo	22 Jul 1994
4:17.00	Natalya Artyomova	Russia	Barcelona	20 Sept 1991
4:16.71	Faith Kipyegon	Kenya	Brussells	11 Sept 2015
4:16.71	Mary Slaney	USA	Zürich	21 Aug 1985
4:15.8	Natayla Artyomova	Russia	Leningrad	5 Aug 1984
4:15.61	Paula Ivan	Romania	Nice	10 Jul 1989
4:14.30	Genzebe Dibaba	Ethiopia	Rovereto	6 Sept 2016
4:12.56	Svetlana Masterkova	Russia	Zürich	14 Aug 1996

1996 was a very good year for Masterkova. She claimed the mile world record, the 1,000 m world record in 2:28.98 and won gold at the 800 m and 1,500 m in the Atlanta Olympics. Dogged by injury in the following seasons, she was never able to repeat her stellar year, although she did win gold medals in the 1998 European Championships and 1999 World Championships.

WORLD TRACK RECORDS FOR THE MILE - MEN

Time	Name	Nationality	Race location	Date
3:46.24	Hicham El Guerrouj	Morocco	Oslo	28 Jul 2000
3:45.96	Hicham El Guerrouj	Morocco	London	5 Aug 2000
3:45.64	Hicham El Guerrouj	Morocco	Berlin	26 Aug 1997

3:45.19	Noureddine Morceli	Algeria	Zürich	16 Aug 1995
3:44.95	Hicham El Guerrouj	Morocco	Rome	29 Jun 2001
3:44.90	Hicham El Guerrouj	Morocco	Oslo	4 Jul 1997
3:44.60	Hicham El Guerrouj	Morocco	Nice	16 Jul 1998
3:44.39	Noureddine Morceli	Algeria	Rieti	5 Sept 1993
3:43.40	Noah Ngeny	Kenya	Rome	7 Jul 1999
3:43.13	Hicham El Guerrouj	Morocco	Rome	7 Jul 1999

While clearly a mile specialist, El Guerrouj was also able to turn his feet to longer distances, claiming the 1,500 m world record in 1998 in a time of 3:26.0, which remains unbeaten, and he holds seven out of the all-time top ten fastest times ever run. He also holds the 2,000 m record in 4:44.79, was a double gold winning Olympic champion in the 2004 Athens Games and received seven golds at the World Championships ranging from Barcelona in 1995 to Paris in 2003. In 2004, he became the first runner to win gold in the 1,500 m and 5,000 m at the same Olympics since Paavo Nurmi's record back in 1924.

JUST FOR THE PROS?

Well, no. Whilst mile races are not so frequently staged as races of other distances, they are out there. The Queen Street Golden Mile in Auckland, New Zealand, was first run in 1972 and was won by Tony Polhill in 3:47.6, beating the then track world record of 3:51.1, held by Jim Ryun of the USA. In 1982, Steve

Scott's winning time of 3:31.25 was 16 seconds quicker than Seb Coe's track world record of 3:47.33. In 1983, the *Guinness Book of Records'* fastest mile was recorded in the race, as Mike Boit of Kenya ran in 3:28.36, which still eclipses Hicham El Guerrouj's track record. Christine Hughes won the women's event in 1983 in 4:02.93, which still beats the track record of 4:12.56 set by Svetlana Masterkova in 1996. The reason for such fast times? The race is run on a ridiculously steep downhill street. In 2013, the organisers allowed a small number of non-professional athletes to enter, with parachutes, soundness of mind and first-aid experience being optional.

THE OTHER WAY

Hills aren't always a guarantee for a quick time. In 2012, the first runner home in the Ilkley mile race took an apparently leisurely 7.29, whilst last place was 17.22. The fact that it was all uphill might have had something to do with it.

THE ANTARCTIC MILE

Set up alongside the Antarctic Ice Marathon, this little fun run a few hundred miles from the South Pole is a tad chilly and isolated. The entry fee of €10,500 and five days in the Antarctic makes the Ilkley race a little more accessible.

CHEATERS AND RULE BENDERS

● ●

❝ Each of us has been put on earth with the ability to do something well. We cheat ourselves and the world if we don't use that ability as best we can. ❞

GEORGE ALLEN SR, US SENATOR AND LAWYER

CHEATERS NEVER PROSPER

It is a sad fact that in professional sport, there will always be people who will try to gain an unfair advantage over their rivals. Athletics isn't immune to the use of performance-enhancing drugs. Before the fall of the Berlin Wall, East German athletes seemed to be performing particularly well. Afterwards, however, they were queuing around the shattered remains of the wall to complain about the strange substances they had been told to ingest by a state-controlled doping policy, known as State Plan 14.25. This forced the German government to put aside a large compensation fund to meet claims by 193 athletes.

And who can forget the eye-popping, vein-bulging Canadian sprinter Ben Johnson on the start line of the 1988 100 m Olympic final in Seoul, South Korea? Having initially won gold, he was stripped two days later of the medal and two world records after testing positive for a banned substance. Judging by his appearance in the race, it would have been odd if he hadn't been using something. Four years earlier, Martti Vainio's 10,000 m silver was quashed for drug misuse. The once great American sprint queen, Marion Jones, admitted to using banned drugs, was stripped of her five Olympic medals and went to jail for lying to the authorities. Closer to home, Dwain Chambers received a two-year ban for taking an illegal substance, although he was subsequently integrated back into the sport – a decision not met with universal approval. Although athletics does not have a cheat on the scale of cycling's Lance Armstrong, it needs to be vigilant in all areas and make sure its pros remain clean.

WELL-KNOWN RULE BREAKERS

There is no drug-testing policy for the thousands of runners who turn out every weekend for races, as they have much less incentive to take anything in the first place; it isn't worth risking your health to come two hundred and eleventh instead of four hundred and fifty-second in a race. However, there have been runners who have tried to cheat in other ways, both pros and amateurs. In 2009, the Chicago Marathon disqualified 252 runners who missed two or more timing mats, while a year later the New York City Marathon knocked out 71, with at least 46 believed to have not gone the distance. In 2011, one competitor in the Montreal Marathon was disqualified after being caught jumping on a push-bike to make up time.

FRED LORZ

In the 1904 St Louis Marathon, Lorz represented the USA in a race beset by heat, dusty roads and poor organisation. At the nine-mile mark he dropped out and was given a lift by his manager for the next 11 miles until his car broke down. He jumped out and ran the rest, crossing the finish line in first place in front of the probably half-drunk Thomas Hicks. The waiting press took photographs of him standing next to Alice Roosevelt, the President's daughter, who placed a laurel wreath over his head. A race official eventually said he had seen Lorz in a car and the truth came out, after which he claimed that it was a practical joke. He was banned for life by the AAA, but it was subsequently rescinded. He would go on to win the Boston Marathon in 1905, in a time considerably quicker than Hicks' gold-medal performance and the existing Olympic record of Spyridon Louis. (This race also featured Cuban postman Felix Carvajal, who stopped to eat rotten apples in an orchard, experienced stomach pain and had to lie down yet still finished fourth in his adapted street clothes.)

KIP LITTON

Litton, a middle-aged Michigan dentist, is either a much maligned, prodigious marathon runner or serial cheater in a league of his own. Indeed, in one race – the West Wyoming Marathon, which he set up in 2010 – he was in a league of his own as he finished in first place. The trouble was that the West Wyoming Marathon had only one real entrant; all the names that Litton added to the post-race results page were fictitious. It was part of Litton's quest to transform himself online from a decent-but-average marathoner to one who consistently ran sub-three-hour performances throughout the USA. He created a website where he recorded his aim of trying to raise money for cystic fibrosis by running these marathons in every state in America. The website has now been closed down but not before his claims were dissected in minute detail by a cohort of angry runners.

Over the years, Litton has been disqualified by race directors for a number of cheating accusations, including both not actually running the race and taking shortcuts. His modus operandi was to start a race behind the rest of the field, his race number concealed by a sweatshirt and a cap obscuring his face. He would then appear at the end of a race, on occasions in different clothes, without fellow racers or race photographers having recognised him from the course, and timing mats having been missed. It reached a point where so many runners reported not having seen Litton on the courses, that diligent racers across the United States began scouring Litton's race records looking for his timing splits and photographs of him on the course, which were rare. The Missoula Marathon in Montana also disqualified him from his second-place age group finish after the runners in front and behind reported they had not seen him in the race.

The controversy around Litton led to hundreds of online threads on well-known running websites, and began to paint a picture of Litton as a serial fantasist. He broke the unwritten runners' code that to call yourself a marathoner, you have to cover the entire course. By cutting it short, Litton not only cheated himself out of the satisfaction of completing the distance but he also disrespected every other runner who has ever done so, no matter what time they crossed the finish line.

What made Litton's story stand out even more was the extent of the allegations of cheating made against him, and his constant denial despite the weight of evidence accumulated against him. He became such a hot topic in running circles that he was the subject of an extensive and fascinating article in *The New Yorker* in 2012, which highlighted races where Litton had run the second half a great deal faster than the first, commonly known as a negative split. Runners strive to achieve such a split and they are hard to achieve, particularly with any significant time gap. The article reported that such was the difference in Litton's splits that 'a variance of that magnitude is as common as snow in Miami'. It also reported the view of one official race timer who stated, when talking of Litton's apparent powers of acceleration in the second half, that 'I don't know any Kenyans who could do that.' For a time, the internet was awash with debate as to how Litton managed to fool so many race directors, as many of his alleged race times still stand, but it is a secret that Litton has refused to disclose, much to the irritation of many members of the running community. *The New Yorker* observed, 'It came down to this; at the Boston Marathon... Litton had hit every split, changed his clothes along the way and broken three hours. No one but Litton could say how he did it.'

ROSIE RUIZ

The most famous amateur cheat has to be Rosie Ruiz, who came first in the 1980 Boston Marathon in a course record time of 2:31:56. Her lack of sweat-drenched clothes, the fact that she didn't know what 'splits' were, and that the second-placed woman hadn't seen her throughout the race raised suspicion. When two witnesses said she had appeared out of the crowd with half a mile to go, the game was up and the win was awarded to Jacqueline Gareau. Later, a photographer also said she had seen Ruiz on the subway during the New York City Marathon in 1979, a race she had used to gain entry to Boston. Despite the weight of evidence against her, she never admitted to cheating.

ABBES TEHAMI

Algerian runner Abbes Tehami lost the Brussels Marathon in 1991 by a matter of millimetres. Having apparently started the race with a moustache, he finished clean-shaven. Even given his apparent prowess at distance running, that would have been an impressive stunt to pull off. It transpired that his hairy-lipped coach had run the first seven miles (11 km) or so, before swapping with his clean-shaven protégé intent on claiming the prize money of more than $7,000.

> ### FASCINATING FACT
>
> Leading up to the Athens Olympics in 2004, the Greeks had high hopes of medal success in the shape of sprinters Konstadinos Kederis and Ekaterina Thanou. On the day before the Games were due to start, with Kederis lined up to be the flag bearer, both failed to attend a drug test. Allegedly, they had both been hurt in a motorcycle accident and were eventually forced to withdraw from the Games. It transpired the accident had been staged and seven years later they were both criminally convicted and received suspended prison sentences.

THE MOTSOENENG BROTHERS

Whilst not identical twins, Sergio and Fika Motsoeneng swapped places and clothes in a mobile toilet during the 1999 Comrades 56-mile ultramarathon in South Africa between Durban and Pietermaritzburg. They were later caught after a newspaper published a photo of them wearing watches on opposite wrists. Perhaps the most humiliating part is that, despite their antics, they only came ninth. In 2010, Sergio returned to claim third place, only to have his medal stripped and winnings cancelled for using a banned substance.

ROBERTO MADRAZO

Roberto Madrazo was a Mexican presidential hopeful who ran the 2007 Berlin Marathon in a time of 2:41:12, a good enough time to put him into the elite category. His finish photo shows him smiling, arms aloft, crossing the line in a hat, pants and baggy running jacket, barely sweating. The runners around him are in vests and shorts and are on their last legs, as would be expected with such a fast finishing time. It transpired he missed two timing mats, which, on the Berlin course, are just impossible to avoid and 'ran' nine miles (14.5 km) in 21 minutes.

CHINESE STUDENTS

At the 2010 Xiamen Marathon in China, an unusually high number of students from a particular school in the Shandong province clocked remarkably quick finishing times. A high percentage even seemed to cross the finishing line at the same time, frequently three abreast. The answer? A large number had given their timing chips to faster students who would carry two or three at a time, or others hitched lifts in order to try to get a time below 2:34, which would give them extra points for coveted university places.

ROB SLOAN

The Kielder Marathon in Northumbria has a strong claim to Britain's most beautiful run as it is, its website boasts, adjacent to a huge reservoir. It's also tough, involving undulating forest paths, with the last six miles (nine-and-a-half km) taking in some leg-sapping climbs. Perhaps that's why former Sunderland Harrier runner Sloan jumped on one of the shuttle buses waiting at the 20-mile point, hopped off near the end and proceeded to run in for third place. After the real third-place finisher complained he had only seen two runners in front of him, Rob was eventually disqualified whilst still protesting his innocence. He had won a 10 k race the day before in a legitimate time of 38:10. Who runs that fast or far the day before a marathon? No wonder he dropped out. At least the organiser, Olympian Steve Cram, had the last laugh: the website now describes the race as 'tranquil, challenging, rewarding... but no bus ride'.

JASON SCOTLAND-WILLIAMS

The personal trainer caused a furore in the running community after the 2014 London Marathon, when pictures of him holding a finisher's medal that he wasn't entitled to were spread across social media. The problem for Jason was that he ran an unremarkable first half in 2:07:05, before clocking 2:49:46 at 20 km and 3:08:47 at the finish – a time quicker than Mo Farah. Runners reported seeing him taking a shortcut, knocking off around nine miles of the route and missing various timing mats. Despite widespread condemnation, the thick-skinned cheat continued to deny he had done anything wrong, causing more anger. Jason had also entered the 2012 race, where a remarkably similar run occurred. At halfway he ran 2:45:15 and the next 13.1 miles in 1:19:39 with a finish time of 4:04:04. At least Jason was consistent in his cheating. Disqualification followed but not until after Jason's finish pictures had made the national newspapers.

SEEING TRACK STARS?

For years, the world of track and field athletics has been awash with famous household names being banned for using an illegal substance and being allowed back into the sport, such as Dwain Chambers. Jamaican sprinter, Merlene Ottey, won nine Olympic medals, 14 World Championship medals (the most of any athlete) and is ranked in the all-time top ten lists over 60 m, 100 m and 200 m. In 1999, her urine sample tested positive for the illegal anabolic steroid Nandrolone, and she was banned for two years by the IAAF. Back home, the Jamaican AAA found her innocent and the IAAF was forced to reinstate her under a technicality linked to retesting not being undertaken within the required timeframes.

The Russian middle-distance runner Olga Yegorova's urine tested positive for the banned substance Erythropoietin, also known as EPO. As the authorities failed to take an accompanying blood test, she missed a suspension on a technicality. Yegorova would later receive a two-year ban for other offences in 2008, after she had pocketed substantial career winnings. Even the once golden boy of British sprinting, Linford Christie, received a two-year ban from the IAAF in 1999 as he waited to be cleared by England Athletics.

There are many others, but perhaps one that stands out is Justin Gatlin, a 100 m gold medal winner at the 2004 Athens Olympics, former world record holder and world champion. In 2001, while still a junior, he received a two-year ban after a positive test and he was again banned in 2006 for four years. He denied the allegations but it didn't help his cause in the eyes of the public that his coach also looked after heavyweight

FOR THE LOVE OF RUNNING

dopers Ben Johnson, Marion Jones, Tim Montgomery and Dwain Chambers. By the time Gatlin re-emerged from the wilderness he was competing against one of the most revered athletes on the planet, Usain Bolt. Fast forward to the 2015 World Championships and the press went into overdrive, billing the 100 m and 200 m showdown between the two as 'Good versus Evil' – and you can guess who the villain was. The newspaper and television coverage was markedly biased in favour of Bolt, who won both events, cementing even further his saint-like status in the athletics world. Twelve months later and the story was repeated in Rio. Despite Gatlin's years of denial, it is unlikely that he will ever shake off the public's perception of him as a drugs cheat.

NOT AGAIN?

After the East German state sponsored doping programme, there was hope in athletic circles that such widespread cheating would not happen again. While athletics was tarnished by high profile drug suspensions, the likely return to the antics of the East Germans seemed remote. That was until German broadcaster, ARD, made a programme called 'Top-secret Doping: How Russia Makes its Winners'. The World Anti-Doping Agency set up a commission to investigate, which led to Russia's provisional suspension from all international athletics competitions organised by the IAAF in 2015 and the eventual blanket ban from the 2016 Rio Olympics of the entire athletics squad. The IAAF reputation did not escape unharmed through widespread criticism of the way in which it dealt with the claims that Russia ran a systematic, state controlled programme that was essentially designed to cheat. A ban from the Paralympics also followed, leading President Vladimir Putin to say 'The decision to disqualify our Paralympic team is outside the law, outside morality and outside humanity.'

And then there's Kenya with its rich heritage of world-class middle- and long-distance runners. The Rift Valley is one of the best places on the planet to train and the East African nation churns out so many superstars. The problem is that the quality of the athletes is so high, runners who would easily make many other national squads can't break through to the Kenyan teams without performance enhancing substances. Being unable to make it as an elite runner does not give the Kenyans or any other nationality the right to unfair gains over clean athletes. Since 2012, 40 Kenyans have failed drugs tests, all of which is deeply disappointing to athletics fans around the world. Who next? China? America? The Vatican City?

IS IT WORTH IT?

Whatever the length of the race, the satisfaction is in finishing, regardless of time or position. The person who crosses the line in last place has covered the same distance as the winner and will be applauded by their fellow competitors. It takes a special kind of determination to be out there for six-plus hours with eight miles to go, knowing that half the field will already be on the way home and tucking into something hearty. George Sheehan said, 'It's very hard in the beginning to understand that the whole idea is not to beat the other runners. Eventually you learn that competition is against the little voice inside you that wants you to quit.' The majority of runners never step on a podium, bank a winner's cheque or take part for any reason other than they want to do the best they can. Taking a shortcut or swapping places just doesn't make any sense and deprives the runner of the thing that matters the most: the sense of achievement.

TYPES OF RUNNING RACES

* * *

" I always loved running... it was something you could do by yourself, and under your own power. You could go in any direction, fast or slow as you wanted, fighting the wind if you felt like it, seeking out new sights just on the strength of your feet and the courage of your lungs. "

JESSE OWENS, ATHLETE

ADVENTURE vs TRAIL vs ROAD

The runner has an abundance of options to choose from in terms of distance, terrain, adventure and navigation to name but a few. Most will start their careers on the road and might work towards an accessible 5 k at a local parkrun. As fitness, confidence and aspirations grow, runs will increase in length and thoughts will turn towards 10 k races and longer. For many, the certainty of the road is enough; it provides easily measurable distances, an even surface and repeatable routes over which progress can be charted.

New runners tend to focus on time and distance improvements. Whilst that satisfaction remains, with experience they will start to look further afield for different challenges. The world of trail or fell running, self-navigating mountain races, orienteering events, mixed-terrain team relay events, or adventure and obstacle runs might open up new and exciting chapters. For the speed merchants, the 400 m oval track might be their calling. Some will integrate the dark arts of cycling and swimming in triathlon races, although runners often argue that their sport is the hardest, as it doesn't involve sitting down or having a splash at the local pool. The Brownlee brothers may disagree.

FASCINATING FACT

Lucio Fregona won the Fregona Marathon in Italy in 2004 and Helen Clitheroe won the Clitheroe 10 k in England in the same year.

WHICH RACE TO CHOOSE?

There is a burgeoning list of races fighting for the runner's pound every weekend, from 5 k races to marathons and beyond. Organisers have to think of ever-more ingenious ways to entice people to their shindigs, frequently starting with the race name. No longer is it enough to call your race the West Lothian 5 k. Titles such as the Snakes Pit Challenge or The Pain Barrier seek to grab the attention and wallets of weekend athletes, implying the event is tougher than the rest. Why else would a race be called The Ball Breaker, or some other similarly testosterone-charged handle? In recent years, even a fancy title hasn't been enough as discerning athletes have cottoned on to the fact that, despite the name, it is after all just another 5 k or 10 k race.

Smaller events can offer good value for money with lower entry fees, as can races without a large goody bag. Many running clubs put on races for the benefit of their fellow runners in other clubs, who then return the favour by putting on their own events. Inevitably, club events tend to be cheaper than those put on by organisations intending to make a profit.

Avoid being seduced by the title, pick a distance and/or terrain and decide what you want to achieve. If you want a new personal best, stick to the tarmac. If you want to feel at one with nature and forget personal best hunting, hit the trails. If you thrive on exhaustion and don't mind risking injury, try adventure or obstacle races. Whatever the time, distance or ground you choose, remember one thing – you are not just out there jogging. You have become a racer.

ROAD AND TRACK RUNNING

Most athletes will train and race on tarmac at some point or other. While a 400 m oval track is not the preserve of professional athletes, amateur races are rare. There are running clubs throughout the UK which have excellent track facilities, like Biggleswade AC and Inverness Harriers. Some host open track meetings, which tend to attract club athletes to programmes replicating the main shorter Olympic distances. There are notable exceptions, such as the Crawley 12-hour Track Race, which in 2016 saw first-placed Michal Masnik run 83.58 miles (134.51 km) at the front of 22 finishers. The Melbourne Tan Track 100 km Ultra takes place in Australia, whilst the Self-Transcendence Ultra track race in Ottawa, Canada, describes itself as 'the longest-running 24-hour race in the world'. In 2012, Greek athlete Yiannis Kouros ran 136.018 miles (218.9 km) on an indoor 400 m track. But track running isn't the preserve of professionals; with a bit of research, events of any distance can be found up and down the country, or further afield for those who want to pull on their running spikes.

ADVENTURE/OBSTACLE RACING

A typical adventure race will involve two or more endurance disciplines combining foot, pedal or waterpower, and is frequently self-navigating in remote areas. They range from two- or  three-hour sprint races to multi-day events for soloists or teams; the Adidas Terrex Swift, for instance, is a two-day, non-stop event for mixed-sex teams of four, incorporating trail running, mountain biking and kayaking. Events such as the Skibbereen Charity Adventure Race offer three courses to suit all levels, ranging from the 'Taster' – incorporating a 17 km run, five km biking and one km kayaking – through to the 'Expert' with 76 km, 21 km and one km respectively, all set in an area of stunning scenery in West Cork, Ireland.

At the extreme end of the scale is the ten-day Chilean Patagonia Expedition Race, known as the Race to the End of the World, as it heads 351 miles (565 km) towards Antarctica. The route changes every year and attracts an international field, which has included athletes from the UK, Russia, Mexico, Sweden and Kazakhstan. Its aim is to raise global awareness of the fragile, diverse and threatened environment in which it takes place, while at the same time seeking to bring sustainable tourism to the area.

> **❝** *I don't measure a man's success by how high he climbs but how high he bounces when he hits bottom.* **❞**
> **GEORGE PATTON, US ARMY GENERAL**

Obstacle races were primarily imported from the USA in the early 1990s and blend running with all manner of weird and wonderful impediments in races of varying times and distances. The noughties witnessed a rapid increase in obstacle races in the UK, jumping onto the already existing bandwagon of famously difficult challenge events (one of which being the Grizzly Run in the Devon village of Seaton, which has taken place annually since 1988 and relies on good old-fashioned sand, hills and shingle beaches to dish out punishment to its competitors). Events organised by companies such as Rat Race or Tough Mudder throw in all manner of obstacles along the way. They also follow the unwritten rule that the harder the race, the more extreme the title needs to be, implying that the combatants will be faced with life-threatening experiences, momentous hurdles and almost insuperable challenges. The Spartan Beast or Tough Guy claim to be the hardest events in the world, and such titles tell the competitor that if they finish, not only will they have entered the lion's den, but they will have looked in the lion's mouth and flossed its teeth.

It's unlikely that a 12-km or 20-mile cross-country affair – which combines running, mud baths, fire, rivers, cycling, straw bales, kayaking and 10,000 volts of electricity to negotiate – will make it to the Olympics. But that's not going to deter the Indiana Jones types who find it impossible to readjust to a standard running race. Once they have crossed the threshold, it's hard to come back.

The public's desire for something different to road racing has underpinned the popularity and continued growth of these races in recent years and their tamer cousins – exercise boot camps. At a basic level, these types of events share the same intrinsic physical and psychological skills needed by anyone who takes part, as aerobic fitness and body strength combine with mental toughness.

TRAIL, FELL AND MOUNTAIN RUNNING

It's tempting to think that when astronaut Neil Armstrong said, 'I believe that the good lord gave us a finite number of heartbeats and I'm damned if I'm going to use up mine running up and down a street,' he was actually promoting the benefits of trail, fell or mountain running. Hewn from the same tree, all are off-road routes on natural terrain and frequently involve self-navigation. Those who undertake them generally don't do it for quick times, as trail marathons tend to take longer than their road equivalents.

Trail running is accessible even for committed urbanites. Britain has many long-distance paths running all over the country, such as the 1,400 km All Wales Coast Path, the 160 km South Downs Way – which hosts many good running events on its tough, undulating trails – the 176 km Cleveland Way or the 80 km Moray Coast Trail in Scotland. The country is crossed with local paths and trails offering runners the chance to escape the hardness of the pavement. It provides softer ground – which helps with injury prevention – and lets runners see things they might not otherwise.

The sight of a nesting osprey searching for food for its chicks just off a woodland trail in the middle of Scotland; the views from Snowdon; being stuck knee-deep in a bog in a desolate section of the North York Moors; or running through the night on trails using head torches and feeling the warmth of the sun on your face as it rises at 4 a.m. don't tend to be the experiences of an average road runner.

Fell and mountain running take place all over Britain and Ireland on steep, uneven ground where the hills are part and parcel of the experience. The Fell Runners Association categorises races by the amount of ascent and descent, from walkers' classes to the category MM, mountain marathons, which are multi-day events – often in bleak, wild areas – where competitors, who usually enter in twos, have to carry all their food and camping equipment.

Sound like it's up your fell? Why not try one of the world's best known events in trail terms, the Original Mountain Marathon (OMM). The OMM organises events around the world, including Shinano-Ōmachi, Japan, and Glentrool in the Galloway Mountains, Scotland. An OMM event offers, according to its website, 'two days of endurance, teamwork and mountain skills, held in some of the most remote locations in the world at a time of year when conditions can be extremely challenging.' The advertising is understating what is likely to lie in wait for the brave or foolhardy who venture out into the wilderness. Trails, bog, mud, tussocks (which aren't Scottish footwear), track, heather, scree, rock, grass, forest and rivers are just some of the elements in store. Add in rain, sleet and high winds over a mountain course of 80 km and boy, you have one heck of a fabulous weekend challenge. Good footwear and the best wind- and rain-proof gear that you can afford is essential, although its unlikely to fully protect you. An entrant needs the ability to put up a small tent with their teammate after a long, cold day on the course. A restless night often follows as you try to find a patch of ground to lie on without loose stones. Then, what feels like only minutes later, rain hammering on the tent wakes you and beckons the start of a second full-on day's challenge.

Why do it, you may ask? To feel alive, and to complete an extraordinarily difficult physical and mental challenge. To connect with nature and the elements in a way you can't when you are tucked up at home in the warm and dry. To ask yourself the question, 'can I go on?' when your hands are numb with the cold, legs are weary from effort and self-doubt abounds... and then find out the answer. The day after the race you may be cooped up in an office, warehouse or shop and staring at the walls, wondering why management have turned up the heating whilst dreaming of your next great wilderness challenge. As Rudyard Kipling wrote:

> *If you can fill the unforgiving minute,*
> *With sixty seconds' worth of distance run*
> *Yours is the Earth and everything that's in it,*
> *And which is more, you'll be a man my son!*

24-HOUR FELL-RUNNING CHALLENGES IN THE UK

TYPES OF RUNNING RACES

The Ramsay Round, Scotland – 24 summits over 56 miles (90 km), with climbs of around 28,500 ft including Britain's highest peak (Ben Nevis) and 23 Munros (which are climbs of over 3,000 ft)

The Bob Graham Round, England – runners have to bag 42 separate Lakeland peaks on a fixed circuit over 72 miles (116 km)

The Paddy Buckley Round, Wales – a circular route over 62 miles (100 km), taking in 47 summits, and including Snowdon and the Carneddau mountain range, starting and finishing in Llanberis, where the separate Snowdon Marathon also finishes

The Wicklow Round, Ireland – another looped course, over 62 miles (100 km) long and with a punishing 6,000 m of climbing. The route was run by Eoin Keith on the 30 May 2009 in an astonishing 17:53:45, over 1:45:00 quicker than the previous record

---

FASCINATING FACT

American Terrence Stanley holds the record for the longest gap between winning the same race twice, having won the Erie Marathon in 1977 and again in 2005.

There are many different types of running and racing experiences on offer to athletes of all abilities. Stepping outside of your comfort zone and trying a new type of running event could open a new world of adventure, travel and fun. If you don't try, you will never know what you are missing.

PARKRUNS

> **❝** *It's about bringing adults and children of all ages, backgrounds and abilities together. It doesn't matter if they have run for 50 years or five minutes. The beauty of parkrun is in the building of friendships and the sense of community. The events provide an opportunity to learn from other people, to find support and encouragement and to provide that support and encouragement to others.* **❞**

CHRISSIE WELLINGTON, IRONMAN TRIATHLON CHAMPION AND JUNIOR PARKRUN MENTOR

THE PARKRUN COMMUNITY

The parkrun events are free, weekly, timed, mostly Saturday-morning 5 k runs held, at the time of writing, in 417 locations around the UK, as well as venues in Australia, Denmark, Canada, Iceland, Ireland, Italy, France, New Zealand, Poland, Russia, Singapore, South Africa, Sweden and the USA. Founded by Paul Sinton-Hewitt in

2004, the first parkrun (or Bushy parkrun, named after the location of the inaugural race in Surrey) saw just 13 runners and four volunteers take part. The aim was not to create a series of races, but to create runs where people could turn up and do whatever they wanted, with the emphasis on taking part. As its website states, the brilliantly simple concept allows athletes of any ability to run with Olympians, veterans to show a clean pair of heels to juniors and the opportunity for non-club runners to dip their unblackened toenails into low-key fun events. To join the growing throng, a runner pre-registers, prints their own specific barcode and turns up at the event of their choice. There are no queues to collect numbers, pens to be herded into or warm-up routines to undertake with Mr Motivator. Afterwards, a quick flash of the barcode to one of the waiting volunteers to record your time and then it's off to the coffee shop for a well-deserved skinny cappuccino. Results appear on each run's webpage later in the day, with every runner's specific data updated with each new run.

It's a way of life for many, with Saturday mornings inextricably linked to the run, a chance to catch up with friends (or overtake them) and that all-important social cappuccino forgetting the pressures of life for a few, brief moments. Sinton-Hewitt, who was awarded a Heroes of Running Award by *Runner's World* in 2009 and a CBE in 2014, couldn't have foreseen the success of his brainchild. By March 2013, the ever-changing weekly stats recorded that 258,042 runners in the UK alone had taken part in 15,784 events with 2,109,401 separate runs. In just a little over three years, those figures had grown at an unprecedented rate in event entry terms. As of September 2016, 1,071,918 runners had taken part in 69,876 events with 12,006,821 separate runs reaching 60,034,105 km and total hours run equalling 634 years, 233 days, 17 hours, 33 minutes and 34 seconds. By the time you start reading this book, the figures will have changed. Chances are they will have changed again by the time you get to the end.

parkrun is achieving things that the All-Party Parliamentary Group for Running would bite a leg off for, if they could catch one of the runners in the first place. It is bringing new runners into the sport at a rate equal to the running boom periods of the 1970s and 1980s and pulling together members of local communities. parkrun is also entirely dependent on the goodwill of volunteers who run their local races week in, week out. Without them, it couldn't exist, as over 7,000 volunteers are needed each and every week. It has also joined forces with GoodGym, providing even more opportunity to combine physical exercise and volunteering for the good of the community. For instance, following the 2016 launch of the partnership between parkrun and GoodGym, a group ran to a local cemetery to clear ivy and to plant 1,500 bulbs. If you have never volunteered before, take the time to do so. It is hugely inspiring to watch such a wide spectrum of athletic ability taking part, it makes you feel good for doing very little and, in the case of parkrun, it gives you the excuse to join the throng for a brew and chat after the race, even without the calorie-burning exercise.

parkrun has an eye to the future with their junior series, which provides 2 k Sunday runs for children aged between four and fourteen. The aim is to have fun and join in, whatever your pace. The juniors can participate in the Saturday runs as well, allowing the whole family to get the weekend off to a flying start.

FASCINATING FACT

As of the start of 2017, Paul Sinton-Hewitt (see p.151) had taken part in 316 parkruns at 153 different locations – including two on 1 January and 73 others at Bushy parkrun where it all began. He has a personal best time of 18:22, has come first once and pops up in the top ten frequently.

The parkrun central database doesn't provide average race times, although it does update the fastest male, fastest female, most first places, average runs per athlete and PBs, providing both the serious and casual runner alike with the chance to monitor their progress. To encourage runners, they have clubs and milestone T-shirts for runners who reach 50, 100, 250 and 500 parkruns. For juniors, there are T-shirts for reaching ten runs, and clubs for those who run further: a half marathon (11 runs or more), marathon (21 runs or more) and ultramarathon (50 runs or more). In December 2016, the leading junior was Hannah Bloxsidge, who had completed a highly impressive 161 junior runs and seven senior ones.

INSPIRATIONAL PARKRUNNERS

Eight-year-old Bailey Matthews, who has cerebral palsy, completed the Castle Howard triathlon, and posted a video of himself in the final straight abandoning his walking frame, falling, getting up and crossing the line. In that moment, he encapsulated everything an athlete needs: drive, ambition and a willingness to tackle head-on anything that gets in their way. Matthews is a regular Clumber Park parkrunner, and it must be as inspiring lining up next to him as it would any international athlete. Worth a trip to Clumber Park for that reason alone.

Then there are parkrunners who take the challenge to an extreme, like Andy Collins who, in August 2016, decided to add an extra dimension to his local parkrun event in Tring by running 100 k around the same course to coincide with its hundredth event. His first lap of an eventual 20 began on a Friday at 7:30 p.m. and his final lap coincided with the start of the event the next morning at 9 a.m. The course included long sections in the woods and, while he had company on some of the laps, he was often on his own in the dark during the wee small hours. The event homepage asserts that he burned almost 10,000 calories, ran 101.3 k, climbed the equivalent of 1,707 m and took 15 hours and 11 minutes to do so. And the reason he did it? To raise £1,700 to purchase a parkrun defibrillator for the benefit of his fellow runners, which, on that course, is highly sensible forward-planning. Post the final lap, Collins didn't need to settle for the low fat, skinny option. Instead, he chose a bottle of a locally produced Side Pocket beer. Even at 10 a.m. that was fully justified.

Sometimes it's the people no one imagines anything of who do the things that no one can imagine.
ATTRIBUTED TO ALAN TURING, ENIGMA CODE BREAKER

THE VISIONARY

There are races, such as the Boston Marathon, that have stood the test of time and have been going for many years, but these are usually individual races, distinct and separate from others of their ilk, with their own peculiar attractions. The phenomenon of parkrun, however, is down to one man, Sinton-Hewitt, Commander of the Order of the British Empire, whose vision created the biggest and most unique running movement the world has ever seen.

There are so many races to choose from worldwide that race directors often have to create a unique selling point for their race to stand out from the crowd. The parkrun philosophy was shaped by Sinton-Hewitt who, from the very first run, aimed to provide a free, weekly 5 k run for all without the need for participants to sign their life away, provide medical certificates or reach a qualifying standard. As parkrun expanded with their second event at Wimbledon Common in 2007 – and later that same year into Richmond, Banstead, Leeds and Hyde Park – that simple philosophy has remained at the core of the events ever since. Turn up at a parkrun in Pierre-de-Bresse, France, Sosnovka Park in St Petersburg, Russia, or Rietvlei Farm, South Africa, and you will get the same parkrun values. It makes no difference where you finish, or whether you are pushing a child in a buggy or running with Fido. Open up a parkrun webpage for any other country and the layout of the homepage is, at first glance, almost identical, with the only difference being the statistics at the bottom of each page (which in themselves make fascinating reading). The message is still the same: join the community for a free, no-pressure running event on a

Saturday morning and head for a coffee after, be that at the Drift Coffee shop (Australia), Fosters market (USA) or Tobi's Café (Denmark).

The volunteers adopt the same principles the world over, and the only thing that might differentiate them from another country's is their names, so thank you Handschumacher Rousseaux, Vladislave Panyuhina, Jesper Mortensen and the thousands like you around the world that contribute to the parkrun success. It seems that parkrun not only offers fitness, inclusivity, friendship and philanthropy but also the chance to perform miraculous deeds – and all for free. What's not to love about that?

THE 5s AND 10s

> *What distinguishes those of us at the starting line from those of us on the couch is that we learn through running to take what the days gives us, what our body will allow us, and what our will can tolerate.*
> **JOHN BINGHAM, RUNNER AND AUTHOR**

5 AND 10 Ks AND THE REST OF US

The 5,000 m and 10,000 m are primarily track-based events. For non-professionals, their first introduction to racing is likely to be at 5 k or 10 k events, on road or trails. A 5 k race equates to 3.1 miles and is far enough to provide a challenge yet not so far as to discourage, unless someone mentions that's 14 times around an average-sized rugby pitch. Events are held all over the UK every single weekend and bank holiday, even on Christmas Day before the sherry and three-week-boiled Brussels sprouts are consumed. Trionium's Box Hill Knacker Cracker 10 k on 1 January is a great hangover challenge. As the organisers say, 'You'll laugh. You'll cry. You'll hurl.' And all in fancy dress.

BACK IN THE DAY

By the time of the XV Olympiad in 720 BC, a third footrace called the *dolichos* was introduced to the still-limited athletic programme. Historians believe it to have been between 18–24 laps of the stadium at Olympia, amounting to around 5,000 m. Competitors started and finished in the stadium, with the middle section run in the grounds, passing statues such as Nike near the temple of Zeus. It seems a version of Nike has been with the Olympic Games ever since. The 5,000 m race predates almost every modern racing distance, with the marathon not even making the podium until 1896.

THE FLYING FINNS

The 10,000 m first appeared in the 1912 Olympics. In this and the Games that followed, the event was dominated by a succession of runners from Finland nicknamed 'the Flying Finns'. The first of the Flyers was Hannes Kölehmainen who won three gold medals at the 1912 Games breaking two world records in the process. Had the 1916 Games not been cancelled he may well have become the first double doubler, winning both the 5,000 m and 10,000 m at more than one Games. Kölehmainen turned to the road, winning the 1920 Olympic marathon. In 1920 it was Paavo Nurmi's turn and in 1924, the handle was passed to Ville Ritola who, in winning 10,000 m gold, broke his own previous world record by 12 seconds. He also won the 3,000 m steeplechase, 3,000 m track and was part of the victorious Finnish Cross Country team, and came second in the 5,000 m. Nurmi then returned to win the 10,000 m again in 1928.

In 1932 the Finns were pushed into second and third spots in the race by Janusz Kusociński from Poland, before claiming the full array of medals on offer at the 1936 Games led by Ilmari Salminen.

The Finns' domination extended to the 5,000 m, with Kölehmainen being the first man to double up and win both events at the same Games. At the time of writing, there have only been seven men who have accomplished this feat. Nurmi won silver in 1920 and 1928, and gold in 1924 with a new world record. Ville Ritola won silver in 1924 and gold in 1928. Lauri Lehtinen took gold in 1932 – with Lauri Virtanen taking bronze – and silver in the next Games behind Gunnar Höckert. The war interrupted their dominance and the Finns had to wait until 1972 before Lasse Virén became the second Finn and only the fourth man in history to win both the 5,000 m and 10,000 m golds at the same Games. He repeated the feat in 1976 making him the first double doubler in history. Mo Farah became the second double doubler in history in 2016 at the Rio de Janeiro Games, having previously won the 5,000 m and 10,000 m at the London Games in 2012.

OLYMPIC 10,000 M
GOLD MEDAL WINNERS

Men Women

Date	Runner	Nationality	Time
1912	Hannes Kölehmainen	Finland	31:20.8
1920	Paavo Nurmi	Finland	31:45.8
1924	Ville Ritola	Finland	30:23.2
1928	Paavo Nurmi	Finland	30:18.8
1932	Janusz Kusociński	Poland	30:11.4
1936	Ilmari Salminen	Finland	30:15.4
1948	Emil Zátopek	Czechoslovakia	29:59.6
1952	Emil Zátopek	Czechoslovakia	29:17.0
1956	Vladimir Kuts	Russia	28:45.59
1960	Pyotr Bolotnikov	Russia	28:32.18
1964	Billy Mills	USA	28:24.4
1968	Naftali Temu	Kenya	29:27.40

1972	Lasse Virén	Finland	27:38.35
1976	Lasse Virén	Finland	27:40.38
1980	Miruts Yifter	Ethiopia	27:42.69
1984	Alberto Cova	Italy	27:47.54
1988	Brahim Boutayeb	Morocco	27:21.46
	Olga Bondarenko	Russia	31:05.21
1992	Khalid Skah	Morocco	27:46.70
	Derartu Tulu	Ethiopia	31:06.02
1996	Haile Gebrselassie	Ethiopia	27:07.34
	Fernanda Ribeiro	Portugal	31:01.63
2000	Haile Gebrselassie	Ethiopia	27:18.20
	Derartu Tulu	Ethiopia	30:17.49
2004	Kenenisa Bekele	Ethiopia	27:05.10
	Xing Huina	China	30:24.36
2008	Kenenisa Bekele	Ethiopia	27:01.17
	Tirunesh Dibaba	Ethiopia	29:54.66
2012	Mo Farah	Great Britain	27:30.42
	Tirunesh Dibaba	Ethiopia	30:20.75
2016	Mo Farah	Great Britain	27:05.17
	Almaz Ayana	Ethiopia	29:17.45

DOUBLE TOP FOR THE MATCH

Extraordinarily, women didn't have a 5,000 m at the Olympics until 1996, after the 3,000 m was introduced for the first time in 1984. Tirunesh Dibaba was the first woman to win both 5,000 m and 10,000 m events at the same Games, which she did in 2008. She also ran a world record of 14:11.15 in a separate race in Oslo on 8 June that year, over 25 seconds quicker than Kölehmainen back in the day.

In the 2016 Rio de Janeiro Games, Almaz Ayana won the 10,000 m in a world record time of 29:17.45, over 15 seconds ahead of the second place runner. Her dominance in the race led many commentators to predict she would do the same in the 5,000 m just eight days later in the Olympic stadium. On the day she did indeed cruise to the front, and Ayana looked odds-on to repeat her performance by establishing a commanding 40 m lead in the mid-section. But with 600 m to go she was overhauled by the eventual race winner, Vivian Cheruiyot, and silver medallist Hellen Obiri.

DOUBLERS – MEN 5,000 M GOLD MEDAL WINNERS

Date	Runner	Nationality	Time
1912	Hannes Kölehmainen	Finland	14:36.6
1952	Emil Zátopek	Czechoslovakia	14:06.72
1956	Vladimir Kuts	Russia	13:39.86
1972	Lasse Virén	Finland	13:26.42
1976	Lasse Virén	Finland	13:24.76
1980	Miruts Yifter	Ethiopia	13:20.91
2008	Kenenisa Bekele	Ethiopia	12:57.82
2012	Mo Farah	Great Britain	13:41.66
2016	Mo Farah	Great Britain	13:03.30

DOUBLERS – WOMEN 5,000 M GOLD MEDAL WINNER

Date	Runner	Nationality	Time
2008	Tirunesh Dibaba	Ethiopia	15:41.40

FASCINATING FACT

Charles Olemus of Haiti ran the slowest 10,000 m of all time at the Olympics in 1972, finishing his heat in 42:00.11, 14 minutes behind the winner. He ran the last six laps on his own and delayed the whole track and field schedule. Another Haitian, Dieudonné LaMothe, finished last in the 5,000 m at the 1976 Olympics in Montreal.

AND ON EVERY WEEKEND THOU SHALT RACE

Let your eyes look directly forward, and your gaze be straight before you. Keep straight the path of your feet, and all your ways will be sure.
PROVERBS 4:25-26

The oracle of running, *Runner's World*, advertised 557 separate 5 k races and 852 10 k races in 2013: by 2016 the number of races had grown at a staggering rate with over 750 5 k events on offer and in excess of 1,100 10 k races.

But there are many more 5 k and 10 k events in the UK than those just advertised in *Runner's World*. In recent years, the parkrun phenomenon has swept the nation and the world. The women's running scene has also improved: the Race for Life series, Running4Women 8 k and 10 k races and the Bupa Great Women's 10 k have given women of all abilities the chance to run or walk these distances under no pressure. Organisations like the RNLI rely on the donations from runners who enter their events. Many charities actively encourage participants to dress up and have fun whilst running. It is very entertaining for runners and spectators alike to watch 300 humans wearing antlers, a red nose and reindeer T-shirts struggling through the mud in the grounds of Woburn House in the depths of winter watched by herds of deer; or 700 Santas wearing only hats and Speedo swimming trunks in freezing weather, hurtling down the road in Boston, Massachusetts. It's hard to achieve a personal best wearing a snowman costume.

FASCINATING FACT

Mike McLeod secured a world record in 1989 for the longest winning streak in the same event, having come first 16 times in a row in the Saltwell Harriers 10 k.

MORE PAIN, PLEASE?

Running is like mouthwash: if you can feel the burn it's working.

BRIAN TACKETT, ATHLETE

Don't be deceived into thinking shorter distances are easy, particularly if a personal best is on the menu. Most runners will eventually experience the pain of racing in some form or other, no matter what their distance or pace. One person's energy threshold might not be reached until mile 20 of a marathon, whilst another's might be in the middle of a 5 k race. When reached, the feeling of exhaustion, of legs so heavy that it's difficult to put one foot in front of the other and the feeling of lungs bursting at the seams will make the finish line appear even further away than it is. Varying the race distance will affect the level and type of discomfort that a runner experiences.

The 'gasping for breath' feeling is very specific to 5 k races. In the same way, the depletion of carbohydrates and the explosion of lactic acid in the legs at 'the wall' is inextricably linked to a marathon. Olympian Peter Maher said: 'Running is a big question mark that's there each and every day. It asks you, "Are you going to be a wimp or are you going to be strong today?"' Enlightened amateur athletes know that running isn't about beating others, it's about doing the best they can. The saying 'pain is temporary; glory lasts forever' should perhaps read 'glory lasts until the next race', when another shiny medal can be added to the trophy cabinet that all runners secretly have at home. But any runner who has experienced the discomfort of a race but who still joins the start line of another should recite the words of runner and author, Dr George Sheehan: 'I have met my hero and he is me.'

HALF MARATHONS

··

> *Running is the greatest metaphor for life because you get out of it what you put into it.*
>
> **OPRAH WINFREY, US CHAT SHOW HOST**

HALF HISTORY

A half marathon is 21.0975 km (13.1094 miles), run primarily on roads or trails. It has taken many years for the distance to be standardised, as it did the marathon. In 1898, the Kungsbackaloppet race in Sweden was 27 km and in 1927 Stockholm was 25 km. A 15-mile race started in Waiatarua, New Zealand, in 1943. Races in Kanaguri Hai Tamana, Japan, in 1949 and Paderborner Osterlauf, Germany, in 1950 were both 20 km. The Bernie Hames race in England in 1957 was close at 21.05 km. By the 1960s, races began appearing on the circuit that were the standard distance, like Route du Vin in Luxembourg, San Blas in Puerto Rico and Caesar Rodney in the USA, followed in the 1970s by Hallwilerseelauf in Switzerland. During that decade, the USA, in particular, witnessed an unprecedented growth in accurately measured races.

In subsequent decades, the half marathon has grown in popularity around the world. In 2000, the Broløbet race, across the Øresund Bridge in Sweden, had an estimated world record 79,719 finishers. The bridge was opened in 2000; it spans eight kilometres of open water over the Baltic and North Seas and connects Copenhagen, Denmark, and Malmö, Sweden. Media reports at the time suggested that there would be in excess of 100,000 entrants to the Broløbet race, and organisers accommodated the vast number by staggering the starting times throughout the day according to ability, country of origin and even postcodes. Guinness World Records currently holds that the largest half marathon finish had 41,615 runners and was achieved at the Great North Run in 2014. It was during the 2014 race that the one millionth finisher crossed the line since the event began in 1981. By 2016, *Runner's World* advertised over 350 half marathon races in the UK alone, with many more not on their list.

Some of the larger events offer facilities for wheelchair athletes to race, such as the Great North Run, which saw Canada's Josh Cassidy claim a hat-trick of victories in the 2012 event. Britain's Paralympic athletes David Weir and Shelly Woods had previously won the event four times each. No doubt spurred on by Cassidy's victory, Weir bounced back to win the men's 2013 and 2015 race. Woods went one further, notching up a clean sweep of victories between 2013 and 2015.

FASCINATING FACT

On 19 August 2012, 90-year-old Mike Fremont set a world record for his age, running a half marathon in 2:56:26 in Morrow, USA. On 7 April 2013, the then 91-year-old Fremont set another age world record, running the Knoxville Half Marathon in a time of 3:06:23 to add to the world record he held for the same age group in the marathon with a time of 6:35:47 set in November 2012. Not content with that, Fremont achieved his third world age record as a 92-year-old in November 2014 in Indianapolis with a time of 3:19:40. Equally, if not more impressive, are the achievements of Canadian runner Betty Jean McHugh, who holds nine world records between the ages of 77 and 85, with a personal best of 2:04:19 aged 80. That's right: aged 80 ('OMG', as people 60 years younger than her might say).

The half marathon distance is a challenge that requires training and commitment, but not at the same level as a marathon. It's not so all-consuming, it's less daunting than a full marathon and post-race recovery is quicker. Whilst both distances continue to grow in participation numbers, the half marathon is out-sprinting its rival both in the UK and the USA.

HOT OR COLD?

Further afield the Siberian Ice Half Marathon tests a competitor's stamina and commitment to the cause. The race is held in snowy conditions on 7 January, which is Christmas Day in the Orthodox calendar. In 2016, over 800 competitors ran through

Omsk in temperatures of –24°C, including 34 foreign runners (who had, hopefully, checked the weather forecast before climbing aboard the plane). In something of a contrast, just ten days later, runners could run the same distance in slightly warmer conditions in the Maui Oceanfront Half Marathon, Hawaii. The Russian winners of the snow race, however, were clearly used to the conditions and preferred to battle against the cold than their heat-seeking counterparts. The winner of the men's race, Vasiliy Minaev, crossed the line in 1:08:32 and the women's race Marina Kovaleva in 1:22:3. In Hawaii, Tsukasa Kawarai of Japan ran 1:14:14 and American Lindsey Wilbur ran a time of 1:32:26 in temperatures around 48 degrees warmer than the Siberian race.

THE GREAT NORTH RUN

Former elite athlete, Brendan Foster, created the largest half marathon in the UK, which was first run on 28 June 1981. Twelve thousand runners took part in the inaugural event and it was won by local man and Olympian, Mike McLeod. It has grown to become one of the largest races in the world and attracts national television coverage. In 2016, 55,000 entrants were accepted out of 100,000 applicants, all seeking to run from Newcastle, across the Tyne Bridge and on to South Shields. Along the way, they were treated to a Red Arrows air display, numerous bands and the unwavering support of the crowd that lined the route. Many who run the race do so for charity or in memory of friends and family who have passed away. But all are likely to remember the top-class organisation, world-class athletes, the final mile along the seafront and the camaraderie among the runners every step of the way, be that Mo Farah at the front, winning in just over the hour mark, or Franca Stanners at the back, coming home in 5:02:34 in position 41,315.

GREAT NORTH RUN FACTS

- Kevin Keegan ran the first race in 1981 in 1:26:25

- Steve McClaren took 2:00:10 in 2007

- It takes 37 double-decker buses to take runners' clothes to the finish

- 41 per cent of runners are aged over 40 and 21 per cent 26–30

- By 2012, 846,599 people had finished the GNR covering 11,090,446.9 miles (17.8 million km).

- In 2014, grandmother Tracey Cramond became the race's millionth finisher

- More than 90 per cent of the world's countries were represented in the 2016 race

- In 2016 Mo Farah became the first athlete to claim three straight victories

WINNERS OF THE GREAT NORTH RUN

	Men			Women		
Year	Runner	Nationality	Time	Runner	Nationality	Time
1981	Mike McLeod	Great Britain	1:03:23	Karen Goldhawk	Great Britain	1:17:36
1982	Mike McLeod	Great Britain	1:02:44	Margaret Lockley	Great Britain	1:19:24
1983	Carlos Lopez	Portugal	1:02:46	Julie Barleycorn	Great Britain	1:16:39
1984	Øyvind Dahl	Norway	1:04:36	Grete Waitz	Norway	1:10:27
1985	Steve Kenyon	Great Britain	1:02:44	Rosa Mota	Portugal	1:09:54
1986	Mike Musyoki	Kenya	1:00:43	Lisa Martin	Australia	1:09:45
1987	Robert de Castella	Australia	1:02:04	Lisa Martin	Australia	1:10:00
1988	John Treacy	Ireland	1:01:00	Grete Waitz	Norway	1:08:49
1989	El Mostafa Nechchadi	Morocco	1:02:39	Lisa Martin	Australia	1:10:43
1990	Steve Moneghetti	Australia	1:00:34	Rosa Mota	Portugal	1:09:33
1991	Benson Masya	Kenya	1:01:28	Ingrid Kristiansen	Norway	1:10:57
1992	Benson Masya	Kenya	1:00:24	Liz McColgan	Scotland	1:08:53
1993	Moses Tanui	Kenya	1:00:15	Tegla Loroupe	Kenya	1:12:55
1994	Benson Masya	Kenya	1:00:02	Rosanna Munerotto	Italy	1:11:29
1995	Moses Tanui	Kenya	1:00:39	Liz McColgan	Scotland	1:11:42
1996	Benson Masya	Kenya	1:01:43	Liz McColgan	Scotland	1:10:28
1997	Hendrick Ramaala	South Africa	1:00:25	Luciana Subano	Kenya	1:09:24

HALF MARATHONS

1998	Josiah Thugwane	South Africa	1:02:32	Sonia O'Sullivan	Ireland	1:11:50
1999	John Mutai	Kenya	1:00:52	Joyce Chepchumba	Kenya	1:09:07
2000	Faustin Baha	Tanzania	1:01:51	Paula Radcliffe	Great Britain	1:07:07
2001	Paul Tergat	Kenya	1:00:30	Susan Chepkemei	Kenya	1:08:40
2002	Paul Kosgei	Kenya	59:58	Sonia O'Sullivan	Ireland	1:07:19
2003	Hendrick Ramaala	South Africa	1:00:01	Paula Radcliffe	Great Britain	1:05:40
2004	Dejene Berhanu	Ethiopia	59:37	Benita Johnson	Australia	1:07:55
2005	Zersenay Tadese	Eritrea	59:05	Derartu Tulu	Ethiopia	1:07:33
2006	Hendrick Ramaala	South Africa	1:01:03	Berhane Adere	Ethiopia	1:10:03
2007	Martin Lel	Kenya	1:00:10	Kara Goucher	USA	1:06:57
2008	Tsegay Kebede	Ethiopia	59:45	Gete Wami	Ethiopia	1:08:51
2009	Martin Lel	Kenya	59:32	Jessica Augusto	Portugal	1:09:08
2010	Haile Gebrselassie	Ethiopia	59:33	Berhane Adere	Ethiopia	1:08:49
2011	Martin Mathathi	Kenya	58:56	Lucy Kabuu	Kenya	1:07:06
2012	Wilson Kipsang	Kenya	59:06	Tirunesh Dibaba	Ethiopia	1:07:35
2013	Kenenisa Bekele	Ethiopia	1:00:09	Priscah Jeptoo	Kenya	1:05:45
2014	Mo Farah	Great Britain	1:00:00	Mary Keitany	Kenya	1:05:39
2015	Mo Farah	Great Britain	59:22	Mary Keitany	Kenya	1:07:32
2016	Mo Farah	Great Britain	1:00:04	Vivian Cheruiyot	Kenya	1:07:54

FASCINATING FACT
....

On 13 January 1979, a six-way tie for first place in 1:04:46 was declared in the Governor's Cup Half Marathon.

FASCINATING FACT
....

Current world records recognised by the IAAF for the half marathon are (men) Zersenay Tadese in 58:23 and (women) Florence Jebet Kiplagat in 1:05:09.

UK ROAD HALF MARATHON RECORD REDUCTIONS

MEN

Time	Runner	Date	Race location
59:22	Mo Farah	13 Sept 2015	Newcastle, England
59:32	Mo Farah	22 Mar 2015	Lisbon, Portugal
59.59	Mo Farah	26 Mar 2016	Cardiff, Wales
1:00:00	Mo Farah	7 Sept 2014	Newcastle, England
1:00:04	Mo Farah	11 Sept 2016	Newcastle, England
1:00:59	Mo Farah	24 Feb 2013	New Orleans, USA

HALF MARATHONS

1:01:03	Nick Rose	15 Sept 1985	Philadelphia, USA
1:01:07	Mo Farah	16 Mar 2014	New York, USA
1:01:14	Stephen Jones	11 Aug 1985	Birmingham, England
1:01:39	Geoffrey Smith	25 Sept 1983	Dayton, USA
1:02:36	Nick Rose	14 Oct 1979	Dayton, USA
1:02:47	Anthony Simmons	24 Jun 1978	Welwyn Garden City, England
1:03:40	Trevor Wright	8 Apr 1978	The Hague, Netherlands
1:03:53	Derek Graham	2 May 1970	Belfast, Northern Ireland

WOMEN

Time	Runner	Date	Race location
1:06:47	Paula Radcliffe	7 Oct 2001	Bristol, England
1:08:42	Liz McColgan	11 Oct 1992	Dundee, Scotland
1:09:15	Liz McColgan	5 May 1991	Exeter, England
1:10:59	Liz McColgan	12 Oct 1986	Dundee, Scotland
1:12:07	Ann Ford	6 Apr 1986	Reading, England
1:12:31	Paula Fudge	4 Apr 1982	Fleet, England
1:13:07	Kathryn Binns	1 Aug 1981	Dartford, England

DEDICATION, DEDICATION, DEDICATION, THAT'S WHAT YOU NEED

The half marathon distance attracts runners across the spectrum of athletic ability, some seeking to run as fast as they can and others happy to cover the distance dressed as a character from a Disney film. There are others who seek to combine both and claim their moment in the sun (or rain, sleet or snow) as a world record holder. If they can't compete with the times put in by the likes of Zersenay Tadese or Florence Kiplagat, they can try to cover the distance in a wacky costume.

There are many amazing half marathon records driven by the eccentricity of members of the great running public all around the world. American Brendan Corcoran currently holds the fastest half marathon time dressed as a fireman with 1:48:24, which he achieved in New York in March 2015. Never afraid to shy away from a challenge, Brits have ventured to far-flung destinations to secure some madcap records. In November 2011, UK runner Joanne Singleton travelled to the Schaumburg Half Marathon Turkey Trot in Illinois, USA, to cover the course in a time of 1:35:45 dressed as a strawberry. Obviously. The male equivalent is Jim Heal, who ran 1:22:37 while dressed as a banana (and avoided slipping on the skin along the way).

OUT OF THE ORDINARY RECORDS

Name	Time	Achievement
Andy McMahon	1:27:23	Fastest half marathon wearing a gas mask
Betty Shurin	3:03:48	Fastest half marathon hula hooping
Bridget Burns	1:45:32	Fastest half marathon in an animal costume (peacock)
Jim Heal	1:22:37	Fastest half marathon dressed as a fruit
Justine Galloway	2:46:06	Fastest half marathon running backwards
Lee Riley	1:36:56	Fastest half marathon carrying a 40 lb pack
Michal Kapral	1:20:40	Fastest half marathon juggling with three objects
Tuedon Morgan	62 days 12:58:49	Fastest time to run a half marathon on each continent and the North Pole Marathon

Tuedon's record is a fascinating one, covering each continent and the North Pole in under 63 days. The achievement took a great deal of planning and travelling, deep pockets and an element of luck, and she required race gear ranging from heavy duty wear (to combat the cold of Antarctica) through to lightweight wicking tops to combat the heat of Abu Dhabi.

She completed the races in the following order:

- Carlton Classic Half Marathon (Australia) 2:09:44
- Abu Dhabi Striders Half Marathon (Asia) 2:12:58
- Torcy International Half Marathon (Europe) 2:14:37
- The Carthage Race Half Marathon (Africa) 2:50:57
- Lincoln's Birthday Half Marathon (North America) 2:26:36
- Southern Cross Half Marathon (South America) 2:25:52
- Penguin Half Marathon (Antarctica) 2:58:08
- North Pole Marathon (North Pole) 10:30:49

VERY FANCY DRESS

It is a little disconcerting to be passed in a race by a Teletubby, a giant panda or a postbox but hugely entertaining for the watching crowds and more likely than not their fellow runners. If you have never run down the street dressed in a wacky outfit, give it a try. The shouts from the crowd of 'come on Postman Pat', little children pointing and laughing and the inevitable banter with fellow runners, can turn a race into a happy memory that will last for years. Many aspiring record breakers combine their attempts with raising funds for charities close to their hearts, and even if they don't bag a record they will have had a day to remember. As Ernest Hemingway said, 'When you stop doing things for fun, you might as well be dead.' Time to nip off to the fancy dress shop.

MARATHONS

● ●

❝ *We are different, in essence, from other men. If you want to win something, run 100 metres. If you want to experience something, run a marathon.* ❞

EMIL ZÁTOPEK, OLYMPIAN

HISTORY

The standard marathon distance is 42.195 km or 26 miles and 385 yards, commonly referred to as 26.2 miles.

The race appeared for the first time in competition over 40 km on 10 April 1896 at the Athens Olympic Games, when 14 Greeks and a single runner each from France, America, Hungary and Australia set off to win a silver cup donated by a French philologist, Michel Bréal. Nine finished that first race, and it was won by Greek water-carrier, Spyridon Louis, who took the lead at the 41 km mark and held to the finish. It was a huge spectacle, and Louis finished in the Panathenaic Stadium in front of a packed house and to a rapturous reception. The Greeks wanted to win this event more so than any other, as was plain from newspapers' reports of the day. The excitement was so great when Louis entered the stadium, according to International Olympic Committee reports, that Crown Princes Constantine and George ran to meet him and accompanied him on his final lap. His victory instantly catapulted him to the status of national hero, where he remained until his death in 1940, four years after he was given the honour of being the flag bearer at the Berlin Games. His legacy lives on and his name has seeped into a common phrase used in Greece, '*yinomai* Louis' which literally means 'to become Louis'.

Women weren't allowed to run in that first race – and would not have their own Olympic marathon for another 88 years – although reports from the time indicate that two women named Melpomene and Stamatis Rovithi shadowed the men, or possibly ran the course the next day. Unfortunately, no official records were kept.

Marathons haven't always been the now-standard distance, however, and initially they tended to be around 25 miles, or 40 km. One notable exception was the 1904 St Louis Olympic marathon, which proved to be longer due to inaccurate course measurement. The Missouri City Marathon has, since 2000, put on a yearly accurate race without any reported hitchers claiming top spot (as Fred Lorz had in the 1904 race).

FASCINATING FACT

The Stavros Niarchos Foundation in Athens bought the cup won by Spyridon Louis for a reported £541,250 in 2012 following its sale at Christie's in London.

THE WORLD'S OLDEST MARATHON

The Olympic Committee's spectacle was quickly adopted as the event of choice by the Boston Athletic Association as part of its aim 'to encourage all manly sports and promote physical culture'. The BAA put on its first 39 km marathon in 1897 and it has continued to this day, missing only one race in 1917, making it the oldest race on the circuit. It is many distance athletes' destination race, provided they can make the high qualifying entry standards. In order to gain entry, men aged 34 and under have to have run a previous marathon quicker than 3:05:00 and women 3:35:00, with the qualifying time increasing for runners over 80 up to 4:55:00 for men and 5:25:00 for women. The high qualification standard means that, unlike New York City or London, there is less chance of being overtaken by a giant red phone box or a panda. The terrorist acts at the 2013 race shocked runners across the globe but the aftermath bore testament to the strength of the human spirit, and the compassion of runners and spectators alike.

TOP TEN OLDEST MARATHONS

1) *1897* – Boston, MA, USA   **2) *1907*** – Yonkers, NY, USA

7) *1946* – Belfast, Northern Ireland

9) *1946* – Johannesburg, South Africa

MARATHONS

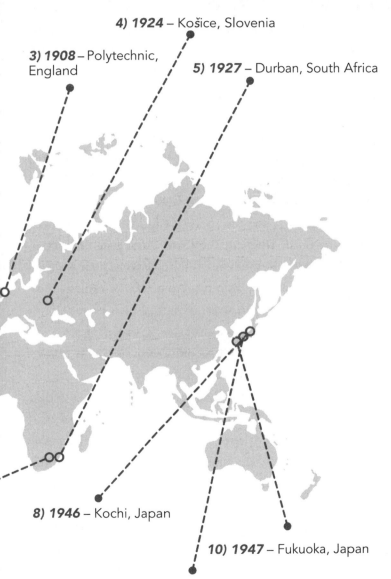

4) 1924 – Košice, Slovenia

3) 1908 – Polytechnic, England

5) 1927 – Durban, South Africa

8) 1946 – Kochi, Japan

10) 1947 – Fukuoka, Japan

6) 1946 – Lake Biwa Mainichi, Otsu, Japan

BY ROYAL DECREE

The 1908 London Olympic marathon was due to finish at the new White City Stadium, built to coincide with a Franco-British exhibition, on an accurately measured 41.84 km (26 miles) course from Windsor Castle. At the request of Queen Alexandra, the start was moved further back to allow children in the nursery to see it, adding in the process an extra 388 yards and dashing the hopes of many would-be sub-three- and four-hour runners in the process. The distance was eventually adopted as standard in 1921 and has caused pain ever since. The 1908 race is also famous as the great Italian runner, Dorando Pietri, collapsed yards from the finish when in the lead. Pietri was the Italian marathon champion and in the lead-up to the race he ran a time of 2:38 in Capri. The race was run on a hot day and Pietri took the lead at the 39-km mark, overtaking the race leader, South African Charles Heffron, in the process. When he entered the stadium Pietri was so confused he didn't know which way to go and collapsed three times. Having been helped over the line he was subsequently disqualified, and the race was awarded to American Johnny Hayes. But the sense of British fair play won over in the end; while he wasn't reinstated, Pietri was awarded a specially created cup by the Queen, who may have felt a little guilty. The extra distance conquered even the professionals. There's hope for us all.

The exploits of Pietri became global news and helped to grow the popularity of the race distance. He was even immortalised in verse in the song 'Dorando' by Irving Berlin, which contains a catchy second verse:

Dorando! Dorando!
He run-a, run-a, run-a, run like anything
One-a, two-a hundred times around da ring
I cry, 'Please-a nunga stop!'
Just then, Dorando he's a drop!
Goodbye poor old barber shop
It's no fun to lose da mon
When de son-of-a-gun no run
Dorando
He's a good for not!

If you check it out on YouTube, beware that the first three lines will stay in your head all day. In 1948, Etienne Gailly almost repeated the events from 40 years earlier. He had led the Olympic marathon from the six-mile mark and when he entered Wembley Stadium in the lead with 400 m to go, he could barely stand up. He was overtaken by Delfo Cabrera from Argentina who would win in 2:34:51 and GB athlete Thomas Richards who claimed silver in 2:35:07. Gailly was exhausted but retained the common sense to avoid help from race officials and gingerly crossed the finish line in 2:35:33. Perry Como might otherwise have had a hit on his hands, assuming he could have rhymed 'Etienne'.

SUNDAY-MORNING FEVER

Marathon running as a recreational pastime spread slowly around the globe. In Africa the Comrades Marathon started in 1921, whilst in Asia the Fukuoka began in 1947. Races sprang up, but they weren't the mass-participation events they are now. In Britain, the Polytechnic Marathon started in 1908 and has been run intermittently since. Others followed, including Ryde on the Isle of Wight in 1957 and White Peak in 1977 – which has a steep, painful downhill section around the 23-mile (37-km) mark – but races were sporadic. It wasn't until the London Marathon in 1981 that long-distance running really started to appeal to the wider British public and only then after a slightly wobbly start.

LONDON'S CALLING

Every jogger can't dream of being an Olympic champion, but he can dream of finishing a marathon.
FRED LEBOW, NEW YORK CITY MARATHON ORGANISER

The success of the New York City Marathon inspired John Disley and Chris Brasher to repeat the vision of Lebow in Britain. Brasher had been mesmerised by the New York City race and wrote about it in the *Observer* newspaper, calling it the 'greatest folk festival the world had seen'. The people of New York had taken the race to their hearts and would come out in their thousands to support the runners. Anyone who has run the race can testify to the generosity of support along the course. The wall of sound that seems to emanate particularly along First Avenue, where the spectators can be ten deep, can be a highly emotional experience. It was this that Brasher sought to replicate. He wanted to raise the standard of British marathon running, give athletes of any size, speed or ability the chance to enter, unite people and create a lasting sporting event for the city.

On 29 March 1981, 7,055 runners, 300 of whom were women, started the first race and 6,255 finished in cold, wet conditions. It was a dead heat between American Dick Beardsley and Norwegian Inge Simonsen in 2:11:40, with Joyce Smith winning the women's race in a British record time of 2:29:57.

What makes London so special? Every single runner and supporter that turns out, and the atmosphere they create. Try catching a 6.30 a.m. train into the City on race day. The excitement bubbles over into animated conversations on normally silent commuter trains, many rehearsing race plans or discussing how many jelly babies to eat at mile 12 or 17.4. What to drink and when (water and sports drinks at different times), what to Vaseline (everything), what to wear (old worn-in gear), how fast to run the first three miles (planned and practised race pace), how many loo stops (shouldn't need them if hydrated properly), pre-race rituals (four visits to the portables) and more are all minutely dissected.

FASCINATING FACT

The Guinness World Record for a married couple running the most marathons was achieved in May 2016. UK runners David and Linda Major ran 1,050 races to reach that milestone. Unsurprisingly, Dave is a lifetime member of the 100 Marathon Club.

TRACKING THE PROS

Many of today's professional athletes start their careers running track, moving onto longer distance road running when their legs cannot carry them around the oval at the speed they once could. There are always going to be exceptions to the rule, like Vivian Cheruiyot a middle-distance track specialist who won 5,000 m Olympic gold in Rio in 2016 and a month later won the Great North Run. Britain's double double gold winner Mo Farah claimed top spots at the London and Rio Olympics and his forte is arguably middle-distance, but he is no stranger to half and marathon road races. In 2014, Farah ran the London Marathon finishing in eighth place with a personal best of 2:08:21. He was the first British athlete to cross the line ahead of fellow GB athletes Chris Thompson in eleventh place and Scott Overall in seventeenth but his time wasn't quick enough to beat the British marathon record of 2:07:13 set by Steve Jones in Chicago in 1985. Farah's fastest half marathon currently doesn't place him in the IAAF top 50 rankings and his London PB puts him even further back outside the top 300 fastest ever times. At elite level the gap is likely to be too much for Farah to ever come close to the marathon world record and he may not even beat Jones' mark. It seems that even one of the world's best ever middle-distance athletes has his limitations.

Those with even greater limitations in distance road events are athletes who specialise in sprinting, which is why the world will never see the undisputable king of the fast twitchers, Usain Bolt, lining up against Farah on the starting line of a marathon. Or even a 1,000 m race for that matter. Bolt can cover 100 m in a time quicker than any human on the planet, but he's not built for long distances. Line him up against Farah and the chances are Bolt will be overtaken by the 600 m mark as his anaerobic ATP-CP system, anaerobic lactic system and aerobic system all run out of gas. All athletes train for specific events and, in Bolt's case, if he turned up at the start line of any marathon, he would be likely to finish in the middle to the back of the masses.

It's not unheard of for sprinters to step up to the big mileage events, like former GB 400 m runner Iwan Thomas who ran London Marathon in 2015 in a time of 4:15:26, firmly placing him in the middle of the pack. In 2016, Dame Kelly Holmes ran a very impressive 3:11:27, but given she was an 800 m and 1,500 m specialist the event suited her more than an out and out sprinter. And who can forget Olympic sprint champion Donovan Bailey taking part in the 2015 Man versus Horse race? The race only covers 21 miles, which he eventually finished in what was believed to be the slowest ever time. And there m'lud, the case rests.

SPRINT DOUBLERS

The following have won gold at the 100 m and 200 m in the same Olympics:

Men

Name	Country	Host City	Year
Archie Hahn	USA	St Louis	1904
Rolf Craig	USA	Stockholm	1912
Percy Williams	CAN	Amsterdam	1928

Eddie Tolan	USA	Los Angeles	1932
Jesse Owens	USA	Berlin	1936
Bobby Morrow	USA	Melbourne	1956
Valeriy Borzov	USSR	Munich	1972
Usain Bolt	JAM	Beijing	2008
Usain Bolt	JAM	London	2012
Usain Bolt	JAM	Rio de Janeiro	2016

Women

Name	Country	Host City	Year
Fanny Blankers-Koen	NED	London	1948
Marjorie Jackson	AUS	Helsinki	1952
Betty Cuthbert	AUS	Melbourne	1956
Wilma Rudolph	USA	Rome	1960
Renate Stecher	GDR	Munich	1972
Florence Griffith Joyner	USA	Seoul	1988
Elaine Thompson	JAM	Rio de Janeiro	2016

WEIRD SCIENCE

Good nutrition is essential for athletic performance and energy is gold. Carbohydrates are the body's most accessible energy source, which is stored as glycogen. Humans can hold enough for around 90–120 minutes of intense exercise, mostly in the muscles and liver. Once gone, the body turns to its fat reserves, which are much less efficient at converting to energy, and hey presto, your legs feel like tree trunks and race pace is very hard to maintain.

When this happens, it's said that you have hit the fabled 'wall'. The rate of reduction of stored levels can be slowed through use of carbohydrate-based gels or sports bars during races and increased levels of fitness. In ultras, particularly of the Long Distance Walkers Association kind, gels and the like are swapped for sandwiches, sausage rolls and cakes. Runners convert glycogen to energy aerobically and anaerobically. The distance specialists train for the former with LSD (long slow distances) designed to push up their lactate-producing threshold and build aerobic endurance, whilst sprinters like Usain Bolt train for short-term explosive power. If Bolt tried running a marathon without changing his training, the chances are he would fall apart and hit the 'wall' like an untrained amateur.

AFRICA – THE MARATHON CONTINENT

At the time of writing, the 75 quickest official men's marathons have been run by either a Kenyan or Ethiopian. Out of the top 345 times, only 67 go to runners from other countries. The only British runner in the list is Steve Jones, who ran a PB at the Chicago Marathon in 1985. Kenyan or Ethiopian women hold 150 of the top 348 slots, although only appear four times in the top ten. British women fare much better than their male counterparts, with Paula Radcliffe holding the top three fastest times ever and a total of nine runs in the list, with Mara Yamauchi and Véronique Marot appearing once each.

GRAND SLAM – THE 'SIX NATIONS' CURRENT FASTEST MARATHON TIMES

Nation		Time	Runner	Date	Race location
	France	2:06:36	Benoît Zwierzchiewski	6 Apr 2003	Paris
	Wales	2:07:13	Steve Jones	20 Oct 1985	Chicago
	Italy	2:07:22	Stefano Baldini	23 Apr 2006	London
	England	2:08:21	Mo Farah	13 Apr 2014	London
	Ireland	2:09:15	John Treacy	12 Feb 1988	Boston
	Scotland	2:09:16	Allister Hutton	21 Apr 1985	London

BIG BUSINESS

Marathon running on a global scale is now a huge, lucrative business. With the ease of access to many of the world's races, the number of participants and finishers continues to rise. In 2011, the New York City Marathon had 46,795 finishers which rose to 49,595 in 2015. London had 36,672 in the same year and by 2016 that had risen to 39,140 runners crossing the finish line on the Mall. In 2010, Chicago had 36,159 and by 2015 that had gone up to 37,437. In Europe the trend is upwards as well, with Berlin accommodating 36,437 in 2015 up from 35,786 in 2008. Asia mirrors the same upward trajectory. In 2007, the numbers finishing Tokyo were 25,102 but by 2016 the number was 34,697. The 2016 Tokyo race recorded 309,824 applications to run, while the earlier version had a much lower 77,521. London 2016 attracted 247,069 applications and 253,930 for the 2017 race. Compare current entry and finisher numbers with early race data and it's easy to understand why there has been a growth in companies providing travel services targeted frequently at the middle-aged marathon brigade in particular. The finisher demographics for the 2016 New York race show the highest age group category finishers was 40–44 with 8,593 runners. Between ages 45–49 there were 7,414 finishers and between 50–54 there were 5,761. The race included 22,824 finishers from 146 different countries around the world, only just lagging behind the home-grown 26,771 Americans. As an aside, males made up 58.3 per cent and females 41.7 per cent of the finishers, while in Japan, the Tokyo organisers need to do something to encourage the women to run: they only reached 21.9 per cent of the total finishers.

FASCINATING FACT

London Marathon entry fees compare very favourably to other big city races, with a huge emphasis on raising charitable funds. These reached record-breaking levels in 2016 at £59.4 million raised in one race, which contributed to a total of more than £830 million raised since 1981.

GLOBE TROTTERS

The club runners and juniors who strutted their stuff during the running boom of the 1970s and 1980s are now in mid to later life. With so many years of running under their Xlite Bumbags, they tend to be the ones looking for new challenges and places to run. As good as they are, once you've run London, Snowdonia, Loch Ness or Dublin marathons or any of the major UK races a few times, a bit of travel and adventure becomes very appealing. Middle-agers plus are more likely to have surplus cash than their younger counterparts struggling to meet the costs of nappies, school clothes and the latest must-have thing. The younger runners still want to take part in the big races, but a combination of lower salaries, higher domestic financial demands and not wanting to leave a young family for three or four days – or not being allowed to – tends to mean that their race adventures are a little closer to home.

Even so, with a little bit of careful planning even those on a low budget can travel to amazing destinations to race. Book early and a flight from Luton airport to Marrakesh, Copenhagen or Paris can be found for less than £60 return, cheaper than a train ticket from the same destination to Chester, Bournemouth or Edinburgh. Each of these cities hold marathons but why go back to race Chester again when you could fly to North Africa at a lower cost?

To keep the other half happy if they are non-runners, save a few Euros and go with running pals and share a hostel room in the Flying Pig in Amsterdam, Archipelago Hostel in Stockholm's old town or Hostel Elf in Prague. Even the hostel names sound more exciting than Premier Inn. In many major cities hosting marathons, the public travel infrastructure is clean, fast, reliable, easy to use and cheap.

Race literature almost always includes an English language version and the organisers do everything they can to make it a memorable experience for the wandering marathon tourist, as they want you to come back to their event in the future. The difficulty they face is that in any major marathon expo before the event, other organisers are on hand to tempt you to their races. This means that Frankfurt, Rome or Seville marathons all suffer the same fate as the races in the UK: why go back when there are so many other big races, all within a few hours' flight time from the UK? With a wee amount of planning they can cost less than a stag or hen do at Chester horse races, which incidentally is the start of the Chester marathon albeit that race doesn't have a stag and hen team category. It's not too difficult to pinpoint why only 23 finished a recent Crawley Marathon, where competitors had to run 105 times around a 400 m running track. It takes a special kind of determination to run a repetitive track marathon and have the ability to cope with the inevitable boredom.

Marathon running hasn't become easier. The distance throws up the same challenges as it has since 1908. Average race times, save in a few categories, are getting faster due to the availability and accessibility of races leading to record entries and finishers.

Perhaps some have adapted Henry V's speech to provide extra motivation to enter:

> *And gentlemen in England now a-bed*
> *Shall think themselves accursed they were not here,*
> *And hold their manhoods cheap whiles any speaks*
> *That ran with us upon London marathon day.*

CROSSING THE LINE

Slower, ordinary, determined people run in races such as the London Marathon with the world's best. They wear Elvis costumes, aim for PBs or just try to finish, or not be outpaced by a hotdog with legs and have feet too painful to walk on for days. Yet every single finisher will share a sense of achievement and pride. They will enjoy the fun, the feeling of being part of one huge running family and the satisfaction that all those months of training have paid off, whatever their finishing time. It feels as though the crowds are cheering every step of the way and, for the most part, they are.

Olympian Sohn Kee-Chung might have been describing his 1936 Olympic win when he said, 'The body can do so much. Then the heart and spirit must take over.' But it applies equally to every marathoner who has ever stood on a start line. Finding the spirit and will to continue when everything hurts (including the bits not Vaselined properly) is an admirable quality. 'You have to forget your last marathon before you try another. Your mind can't know what's coming,' said Frank Shorter. Even the pros hurt and that's what makes the marathon such a personal achievement.

ULTRAS

· ·

❝ People can't understand why a man runs. They don't see any sport in it. Argue it lacks the sight and thrill of body contact. Yet, the conflict is there, more raw and challenging than any man versus man competition. For in running it is man against himself, the cruellest of opponents. The other runners are not the real enemies. His adversary lies within him, in his ability, with brain and heart to master himself and his emotions. ❞

GLENN CUNNINGHAM, US OLYMPIAN

HISTORY

An ultramarathon is, in essence, any distance beyond a standard marathon. Common race distances run are 100 miles (160 km) and 62 miles (100 km) events. Historic ultras were often multi-day indoor track events, popular in Britain and America in the 1870s, run between a Monday and Saturday. Races were commonly known as 'wobbles' and competitors 'pedestrians'. An event of this type is described in Peter Lovesey's book *Wobble to Death*. But the six-day races and ultrarunning in general eventually lost the public's interest and, for a number of years, events were scaled down.

FASCINATING FACT

In 1882, Charles Rowell ran 300 miles on an indoor track in 58:17:06 – a time that has never been beaten.

By the 1920s, interest in the ultra was rising again. In South Africa, the first Comrades Marathon took place in 1921 and the Transcontinental Footrace took place in 1928 in the United States. For many years, ultrarunning was not undertaken by the masses. But judging by the number of ultra events that now take place in the UK and around the world, it seems that this extreme end of the sport has never been more popular.

WHY?

To many runners, a marathon is quite rightly seen as their Ben Nevis, an enormous and yet achievable endeavour. For some non-professional, recreational athletes the distance is just not far enough. Once traversed a number of times, the excitement of a marathon can wane and the endorphins crave bigger challenges. The only way for some to rediscover the buzz is to do something they think they might just be able to do but are not sure – just as they felt when they entered their first marathon. Few runners forget the electrifying mix of nerves, excitement, anticipation and the sense of possibility felt on that first starting line. To recapture that can lead to ever-longer races being entered, as one distance after another is achieved.

The mind of an ultrarunner is moulded by what they have achieved in the past. Very few runners step straight into monster mile-munching without having earned their stripes by conquering the marathon first. Once that particular beast has been vanquished, thoughts turn to the next mountain to climb – the days when 26.2 miles seemed a long way begin to fade into the subconscious, as ever-increasing distance runs take over.

At the 26.2 mile point of an ultra, as runners pass the standard marathon distance, they might be wise to consider the words of Winston Churchill: 'This is not the end. It is not even the beginning of the end. But it is, perhaps, the end of the beginning.' The relevance of those stirring words is dependent on the length of the ultra, as distances vary with every race. A runner covering a smaller ultra, such as the 34-mile (54-km) Greensands Ridge event held in Bedfordshire each June, will see the marathon distance as the penultimate focus point of the whole run. However, an ultrateer running the Montane Lakeland 100-mile (161-km) race, held each July in the Lake District, dare not contemplate it as even the end of the beginning. For very long races, the mind needs to be focused on achievable short-term goals and not the glory of the final sprint finish, 74 miles (119 km) away. Your grey matter cells must be trained to think, and believe, that even running past the marathon point is nothing special. Sixty per cent of an ultra is in the training; 30 per cent in the mind. The rest is left to avoiding rabbit holes, wrong turns and trying to digest all manner of nutritionally bereft foodstuffs to keep you going.

THE WORLD'S LONGEST-RUNNING ULTRAMARATHONS

Race	Distance	Location	Year started
Comrades	89 km (56 miles)	Durban, South Africa	1921
Pieter Korkie	50 km (31 miles)	Germiston, South Africa	1948
London to Brighton	88 km (55 miles)	Brighton, England	1951
Saint Etienne–Lyon	70 km (43 miles)	Lyon, France	1952
Bieler Lauftage	100 km (62 miles)	Biel, Switzerland	1959

JUST A SHORT 26.2 MILES TODAY?

A marathon for the really long ultra boys and girls will turn into a Saturday-morning training run. Anyone fit and determined enough to take on any ultra has to learn to lose focus on the immediate miles ahead. They have to treat the distance with both respect and disdain in equal measure. The running icon, Walt Stack, said: 'Start slowly and taper off,' although he should have also added 'walk the hills'. There is no hiding place in an ultra, no helpful course marshal to push you along when you fade. If you haven't put the miles in and trained properly, you will be found out. Respect the race with proper, focused training in the months leading up to it. Having put the miles in the bank, stick your chest out and tell it that 30, 40 or even 70 miles isn't far and you are going to beat it. If an ultrarunner believes that 30 miles is a long way, they are in the wrong arm of the sport. If they see the last 30 miles as the homeward leg, next year they will be queuing up qualifying points for the Ultra-Trail du Mont-Blanc.

EXCEPTIONS TO THE RULE

There are runners who defy rules and expectations. They might not be famous or known beyond their club, yet their achievements deserve to be heard. Rebecca Fleckney is one such runner who, prior to her club's inaugural 84-mile non-stop John Bunyan trail run, had never run more than a marathon. The event was designed to allow club members to run any distance they wanted between one and 84 miles. She set out with the intention of making maybe 40 miles and ended up covering the lot in a very creditable 24:21:19. How did she do it? By focusing on the next checkpoint and not thinking about how far she had left to go. When she arrived at mile 40, she decided to go to the next checkpoint and then the next until she was so close, no one would let her stop even if she wanted to. She hadn't trained her body for the rigours of that distance but she was able to control her mind.

WHERE DOES IT END?

> " *It hurts up to a point and then it doesn't get any worse.* "
>
> **ANN TRASON, US ULTRARUNNER**

There will come a point, even on the Herculean ultrateer's radar, where the distances become daunting. Even the most experienced recreational ultrarunner is unlikely to reach nirvana in the way the Tendai Buddhist monks in Japan seek to do (which is whilst running up to 51 miles for 100 days in a row, around a sacred trail on Mount Hiei). Spiritual enlightenment and a transcendent state might be achieved by the Holy men, but one has to run a long way to find it.

In one recent 104-mile (167-km) event, the author casually asked a fellow runner how they were finding it. 'Taking it easy,' came the reply, 'I have a 200-miler in four weeks and this is a training run for that.' Putting the Monks to one side, it's good to remember that there is always someone dafter than you out there. Always.

MAD, BAD AND DANGEROUS RACES

••

❝ *Some of the world's greatest feats were accomplished by people not smart enough to know they were impossible.* ❞

DOUG LARSON, AUTHOR

6633 EXTREME WINTER ULTRAMARATHON

This six-day 350-mile (563-km) race starts at Eagle Plains, Yukon, Canada, on the Dempster Highway, before entering into the Arctic Circle after 23 miles (37 km) at the latitude of 66 degrees and 33 minutes, through the Northwest Territories to Inuvik, with a final 120 miles (193 km) along the ice road to Tuktoyaktuk on the shores of the Arctic Ocean. It claims to be the 'toughest, coldest and windiest extreme ultramarathon on the planet', with some justification. Runners are self-sufficient and have to pull sleds with all their gear. Checkpoints only offer water and shelter. Given some are 70 miles (113 km) apart, it's unlikely Domino's will deliver if someone forgets their tin-opener. In 2013, only four out of 20 entrants finished in the perishing temperatures that can reach -44°C. The bite-sized fun run version at 120 miles (193 km) had five finishers out of six entrants. All had to battle against frostbite and hypothermia, dodge aircraft landing on the highway and try not to get lost in the frozen wastelands.

TRAIL OF TEARS 5 K

What's different about this 5 k trail race near to Route 66 and Tulsa, Oklahoma, is the fact that runners wear shoes, socks and nothing else other than a bit of strategically placed Vaseline. Getting back to nature and 'social nude recreation' is the aim of the race. It is one in a series organised by the American Association for Nude Recreation, which includes the Sahnoan Bare Buns Run 5 k, Skinnydipper Sun Run 5 k, Road Kill Run and Bare As You Dare. Racers are ironically presented with race T-shirts and medals, although where they hang them is always a difficult question to ask.

The Americans in particular can't get enough of clothing optional races, with *Runner's World* USA reporting almost 30 different events around the country. Not unsurprisingly, most are in warm states like Florida, South Carolina and Texas, with no current events in Alaska (which, as any male racer who has run clothed on a cold day will tell you, is good news). The Alexandria Beach Carnival in Australia, which began in 1984, involves a naked 2 km 'beach marathon' which requires liberal amounts of sun screen massaged into places that don't normally see the light of day.

The Finnish Nakukymppi 10 k race is strategically fixed near to Midsummer for temperature-related reasons, as is the Roskilde Naked Run in Denmark. The Danish race takes place at a music festival, and the relaxed atmosphere and locally brewed Carlsberg has encouraged a few new runners over the years. In the UK, the Tything Barn 'Bare if you Dare' 5 k has been staged in Pembrokeshire, Wales, since 2002, while the BH5K in Kent allows women to wear sports bras. The organisers also don't object to men using a bit of sticky tape if their appendage might otherwise cause a swaying injury.

An event growing in popularity in the heart of a capital city, is the Streak for Tigers in London Zoo, which raises funds for conservation work and is enormous fun to take part in, even in the temperamental UK climate. Lots of racers cover themselves in body paint and tiger stripes, before embarking on a 350 m streak around the inside of the zoo. Any feelings of embarrassment quickly dissipate, and it's surprising just how many selfies are taken in the buff at the end. The long arms of the monkeys are out of reach, at least of the animal kind.

MUD, SWEAT & BOOBS 5 K

If running in your birthday suit isn't enough, you could always try this American naked obstacle race. It incorporates a number of challenges including:

- Over under stations
- Mud crawl
- Rope ladder

- Rope swing
- Colour pit
- Tyres
- Beer station
- Giant slip and slide

Without trying to put too fine a point on it, there is a danger of picking up a splinter or a burn injury in a delicate area in this clothing optional race.

COMRADES MARATHON

This 56-mile (90-km) road race between Pietermaritzburg and Durban in the KwaZulu-Natal province, South Africa, is the oldest ultra race in the world, the first one having taken place on 24 May 1921. The direction of the race is alternated each year between the two cities, creating 'up and down' years, due to the changes in elevation. It attracts thousands of runners and supporters every year, with over 20,000 people entering in 2017.

It is a cruel race. Competitors have to run the course in under 12 hours to be allowed to receive an official time and medal. One second outside the limit and the chance is gone for another year. It's televised live in South Africa and the last-placed person is celebrated as much as the winner.

THE JUNGLE MARATHON

Set in the Amazon rainforest, this 254-km (157-mile) race is the direct opposite of the 6633. Temperatures climb as high as 43°C, with 90 per cent humidity and some of the creepiest crawlies on the planet. In 2012, 63 runners from 15 different nations battled snakes and avoided jaguars, whilst enduring steep, muddy climbs and dense jungle trying to find the easily missable trails. They crossed swamps and tried not to be eaten by piranhas, all whilst carrying a week's worth of supplies. There are also 42-km (26-mile) and 122-km (75-mile) options. Not one for the barefoot running brigade.

THE ANTARCTIC ICE MARATHON (HALF AND FULL)

Set inside the wilderness of the Antarctic, both races require competitors to face average wind-chill temperatures of −20°C, constant sunlight, and powerful katabatic winds that can reach 300 km (186 miles) per hour. It's too cold even for the penguins, whose march stopped many miles back. Even getting to the start is an adventure dependent on the weather, as the place is officially the coldest on the planet (the lowest temperature ever recorded was -89°C at the Russian Vostok research station).

ULTRA-TRAIL DU MONT-BLANC

Arguably the greatest of all mountain races, the UTMB takes place in the stunning Mont Blanc Massif over a 168-km (105-mile) course with 9,600 m of ascent. It runs through France, Switzerland and Italy, has a maximum number of 2,300 competitors and a cut-off time of 46 hours. There is so much climbing that even mountain goats think twice about following the competitors. It's hard to even enter, as competitors require seven qualification points that can only be amassed by entering other designated trail ultra-distance runs. The organisers do allow these to be accumulated over two years, but even then, entry to the race isn't guaranteed due to the popularity of the event.

FASCINATING FACT

Between 2008 and 2011, Kilian Jornet Burgada won the race three times and held the course record at 20:36:43; the one year he didn't win, the race was cancelled. In 2013, his time was beaten by Xavier Thévenard in 20:34:57; just 106 seconds separated the two men. The following year François D'Haene dropped it to 20:11:44, which remains the current record.

Runners carry a designated kit list, but oxygen bottles aren't compulsory despite runners having to climb the Grand Col Ferret, which, at 2,537 m, is the race's highest peak. Any race where the winner comes in 24 hours ahead of the last-placed competitor is going to be a toughie. If you train for months on end and think you are fit enough for this bad boy, train a few months more and you probably still won't be.

THE SELF-TRANSCENDENCE 3,100 MILE RACE

❝ There is only one perfect road, and that road is ahead of you, always ahead of you. ❞

SRI CHINMOY, INDIAN SPIRITUAL TEACHER

This is the world's longest footrace. The event takes place in Queens, New York, every year over 52 days between June and August. Runners average 59.6 miles every single day, looping a city block measuring 0.5488 miles (0.883 km) a staggering 5,649 times. Great for the spectators, although tedious for the runners, the record was held for many years by German Madhupran Wolfgang Schwerk who, in 2006, reached 3,100 miles in 41 days 8:16:54, beating his previous record set in 2002. The current record is held by Wolfgang Schwerk's arch nemesis, Ashprihanal Pekka Aalto, who ran the distance in 40 days 9:06:21 in 2015, winning the event for the eighth time. They must have run out of things to say to each other at some point.

Created by Chinmoy in 1997, the race distance was upped from the previous year's 2,700 miles (as, clearly, that wasn't far enough). Competitors run the risk of disqualification if they run under 50 miles a day, with a mandatory six-hour curfew imposed by race officials – who probably want to sleep.

The key to Chinmoy's philosophy is the expression of self-transcendence, 'going beyond personal limits and reaching new levels of inner and outer perfection. Whether it be in the athletic world or any endeavour, for someone to transcend his previous achievements is inner progress and an expression of a new determination, which can only bring us closer to our destined goal – real satisfaction.'

MARATHON DES SABLES

Another multi-day event that calls itself the 'toughest footrace on earth' is the Marathon des Sables, a gruelling six-day race in the Sahara desert in Morocco. Created in 1986 by Patrick Bauer, runners' sweat evaporates before they feel it due to the stifling heat, and temperatures reach over 38°C. It is broken down into six stages of differing lengths:

- Stage 1 – 29 km (18 miles)
- Stage 2 – 35.5 km (22 miles)
- Stage 3 – 40 km (24 miles)
- Stage 4 – 82.2 km (51 miles)
- Stage 5 – 42.2 km (26 miles)
- Stage 6 – 21.1 km (13 miles)

The athletes have to carry their own kit, be self-sufficient and have a minimum of 14,000 calories worth of food. In reality, they will need much more than that. Even the mandatory kit list is a sign of just how dangerous this race can be. Runners have to take the following as a minimum:

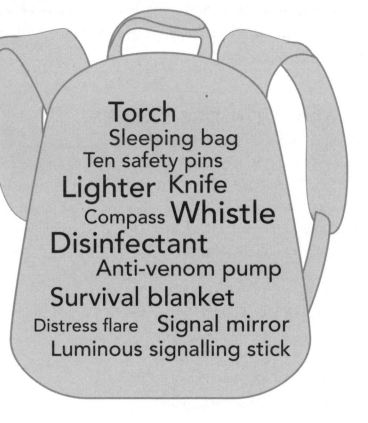

Torch
Sleeping bag
Ten safety pins
Lighter Knife
Compass Whistle
Disinfectant
Anti-venom pump
Survival blanket
Distress flare Signal mirror
Luminous signalling stick

As Morocco is home to 12 different species of snake, ten scorpions and a number of spiders, the survival kit really could mean the difference between life and death. Add in heat, blisters that seem to cover the entire foot, poor food, total exhaustion, disorientation and sand that rips open any chafing injury, and this really is one of the world's hardest footraces.

In 1994, Mauro Prosperi, Italian police officer and former reserve in the 1984 Italian Olympic marathon team, got lost and ended up wandering the desert. He was found nine days later over 100 miles off course, having lost 30 lb in bodyweight. Naturally, having come close to death in the race, he subsequently returned to run it seven more times. Sadly, the race claimed the lives of two other runners in the years that followed Prosperi's close call, including the apparently fit Bernard Julé who died of a heart attack in 2007 following the long stage in which he came forty-fifth out of 750 competitors.

The Olympic rower James Cracknell achieved twelfth place in the 2010 race, giving him the highest finish at that point for a Brit. In 2014, that benchmark was overtaken by Danny Kendall who finished in fifth place just over an hour behind the race winner. Ozzy Osborne's son Jack foolishly attempted to run the race on little training, for his television show *Adrenaline Junkie*. Predictably, he dropped out some way before the end. Rock on, Jack.

THE STREAKERS

· ·

*❝ You only live once, but if you do
it right, once is enough. ❞*
MAE WEST

Did that catch your attention? In the context of running,
a streaker isn't an Erica Roe or Michael O'Brien wannabe
hurtling along a 5 k in their birthday suit. A streaker is a runner
who runs every day (with or without clothes). According to
Streak Runners International (SRI), established 2012, and the
United States Running Streak Association (USRS), established
2000, a running streak requires a run of at least one mile
(1.61 km) within each calendar day. Prospective members can
join the SRI/USRS once their streak has reached one year in
duration and in doing so will add their name to the bottom
of an inspiring list of athletes who have taken streaking to a
higher dimension. As of October 2016, 703 streakers were
registered in categories ranging from Neophytes (under five
years) to The Coverts (45 years plus). It takes some running
to impress this bunch, as ten-year-plus streakers are merely
'experienced'. At the top of the current list of streakers is

Jon Sutherland who, as of 5 September 2016, had run an astonishing 17,300 days (47.36 years) in a row having started on 26 September 1969. He is joined by two others in the top tier, seven in The Legends (40 years plus) and 30 in The Grand Masters (35 years plus). The top 116 have all been running for at least 15 years. Due to the nature of the club, its membership tends to be older although not exclusively. Sixteen-year-old Tarang Saluja has chalked up 486 days, as of 5 September 2016. Just another 44 years to go to join The Coverts.

THE GREAT BRITISH STREAKER

Ron Hill, OBE, began his running streak in December 1964 while he was an elite athlete, and he's believed to be the longest streaker in terms of the number of consecutive days run. At his peak, Ron achieved world records at ten and 15 miles, 25 km and marathon distances, won many famous races including the Boston and Commonwealth Games marathons, raced in two Olympic Games and was the recipient of a host of awards for his achievements as a world-class athlete. Over four decades later, he is still revered by the British running community as a former elite athlete and streaker. His daily running streak has continued despite being involved in a car crash, in which he broke his sternum, and having surgery on another occasion, which led to him running using a crutch. Following his retirement from elite athletics, he added his name to a running clothing range, which includes the classic 1980s Trackster Running Pants.

WHY STREAK?

Running every day isn't a panacea for all known health ailments, a passport to weight loss or a guarantee of increased fitness. Many well-known coaches and athletes alike believe that daily running isn't sensible. Streakers may be more susceptible to common overuse injuries such as plantar fasciitis or shin splints. Running too hard or for long on too many consecutive days could lead to burnout and shorten a racing season.

So, why do it? Non-streakers may struggle to understand the power of the streak, which can become all-consuming, as a runner plans their day around when to sneak in a quick blast or slow slog, where to go and how they can maximise their recovery time. Streaking means that a runner doesn't have to motivate themselves, as every day running is a given. A streaker constantly seeks out new routes, places to run or runners to share that day's workload.

A business trip away or a holiday also provides an opportunity for new and exciting playgrounds to explore. A streaker will happily wander off and explore a new destination by foot power and may well see sights they wouldn't do if they were whizzing by in a car. In the quest for new experiences, a streaker will go out at any time of the day or night, and all kinds of scenes will open up. An early summer morning's run through quiet streets in Lindos, mixing with the locals getting ready for the day's trade while the holiday-makers are sleeping off the night before; a run through Edinburgh on a cold, winter's evening dodging commuters wrapped tightly in extra-thick clothes; a wander along a stony Lakeland trail with just sheep for company; a run along a deserted beach in the middle of a storm so strong that it's a battle not to be pushed into the sea. These aren't runs exclusive to streakers, but if you are on a streak the prospects of sharing these experiences will be higher. Whatever the conditions, a streaker is going out and won't put it off until the next day.

The streak will become a friend, a confidant and something that will never let you down. If you run, the streak will be ready and waiting for you without criticism, without excuse. If you want to do it, the streak will do it with you. The streak will be supportive, it will always be ready to take part in whatever session you want and it will go as far as you and no further. You may have created the streak in the first place, but the longer it gets, the more it will develop a force of its own. Soon, everything will revolve around the streak. Shopping? Sure, but after a quick three-miler. Home from work late and it's dark and cold outside? No problem, where's the head torch? Dinner with friends? If I run to their place, could I use their shower?

A streaker will evolve skills probably never before required. For example, changing from a work suit into running gear in extra quick time in the front seat of a car in a packed supermarket car park, without anyone noticing; the ability to park in a new town, wander off for 5 miles and relocate your car; and slipping in a 4-mile run at lunchtime while everyone else is in the Dog and Badger.

A streak has the power to change priorities, reduce stress and provide a healthy focus away from the pressures of life. It can inspire other runners and help form close friendships through a shared endeavour. Happy Feet Running Group in Bromham, England, only has around 15 active members, but four of those are yearlong streakers who are supported and encouraged by the other members. Mike Thompson and Graham Sturge have even roped in their young children to help keep them going, and they frequently attend Bedford parkrun with their families.

TIME TO CHASE KATHY CHASE

Kathy's story, from non-runner to internationally known streaker is worth a chapter in itself and best told in her own words.

'I had never been a runner and didn't even start until 2010 as a necessity to keep up with a group of walkers training for the Bataan Death March here in New Mexico. They did their long training walks on Sundays and when church services concluded, I would change my clothes and run to catch up with them as their route always passed by the building. After a few weeks, I was hooked on running. I competed in my first race the following May and took first for my age group. I started running regularly to compete in local running events. Six months later, I applied for and was selected to join a group of amateur athletes as a brand ambassador which required me to participate in at least six running events per year and report back with my results. So I increased my training schedule. When the challenge to run every day popped up on Facebook, I figured I was running almost every day anyway, so why not join in the group? I really enjoyed participating and reading about what everyone was doing with their running (particularly one very entertaining runner who shall remain nameless). I vowed that I would finish what I started and push through which I did.

'At the end of 2012, I had quite a sense of accomplishment and decided to continue as long as I could. There were only the four of us still posting runs to the Facebook page at that point, but it was still fun to see what we were all up to. I had also learned something during that first year. Although I had a lot of family and work commitments, everyone I knew had come to expect me to head out for a run, so it meant I got to have a bit of private time every day. No one questioned me or complained, it was just, 'Well, there goes Kathy' and I was off. I have always had a sort of wanderlust during my life, always looking longingly at the trail that goes off into the woods or up the mountainside and wishing I could see what was just beyond the tree line. I never had the opportunity (or made the opportunity) before, but now I had an excuse to explore. I have run most of the trails in the mountains around my home or when we travel, I can say 'I'm heading out for a run', and go where no one else wants to. My husband isn't much of an adventurer and I am. So when he's sitting by a lake fishing (his favourite pastime), I strap on my old running shoes and do my thing. I have run up a 12-mile ski road, around a mountain lake, on the beach in Maui, through the desert and seen views that few people get to see. I've been greeted in the morning by a mama fox and her babies, a pair of coyotes, a skunk or two and the occasional rattlesnake. I've run in the rain, snow, hail and heat (the heat is the worst and I live in the desert). I've climbed up mountains and then run down really fast, run through streams and across dry riverbeds, run across bridges meant only for cars or trains and every time, I've come away with a feeling of accomplishment and wonder.'

Kathy's 2012 streak ended on 8 June 2013 following a bike crash in a triathlon that broke her collarbone. The medical verdict was that she would be out of action for 12 weeks. She was back on the trails within seven and started her second streak on 3 August 2013. Over three years later, and with an excess of 4,000 miles under her belt, Kathy has proven that she's one tough, determined streaker who it's going to take a lot to stop on streak two. As long as she doesn't get on a bike that is.

BY FAILING TO PREPARE, YOU ARE PREPARING TO FAIL

If a runner has been streaking for any period, they can't hang up their daps for a day because they have a cold. The streak would be over and they'd be back to footstep one. The key to any successful streak is planning short-term goals in the weeks or months ahead, and longer-term plans, perhaps to achieve a specific time in an event or a particular running experience. Rest, recovery and sleep are crucial and, while you can't miss a day, there are options. You can run very early one morning and late the next day and create a 30-hour-plus rest period; alternate easy running days with harder ones; keep a detailed mileage log and know your limits, especially at the start of a streak. If you have never done one before, give up on races for a time and concentrate on slowly building an endurance base for the months that lie ahead. Run with others, in different places and listen to your body. If it hurts then ease up. Above all, set yourself a realistic target, which can fit in with your lifestyle. If you previously ran 20 miles a week over three runs, don't aim for 50 miles a week over seven at the start. After an initial surge of excitement, there will be days when it's tough to get out. Know those days are coming – that it won't always be easy – and comfort yourself with the knowledge that, if it were easy, there would be no point in doing it. Be vigilant in the battle against injury, stretch daily and wear out the foam roller.

If a streaker does pick up a niggling injury there are generally two options. The first is to follow sound medical advice and possibly stop running. The second (and more likely to be chosen) option is to ignore that medical advice, adapt the streak to a point where it can continue at its lowest level and plough on regardless. It's doubtful Alberto Salazar would be happy with that, but when a streak has truly grabbed hold of a runner it will take a lot to break it.

HOW LONG?

Only one person can make that choice and that's you. Consider why you want to streak and what you want to achieve. If it's a lifelong daily run, building the miles gradually with low-level mileage while your body adapts is the best course of action. If you want to run for a year, pick four or five events over the course of that year that you can train towards, with increasing levels of difficulty to keep you motivated and focused. Settle on the number of miles you want to run and, right from the start, be consistent with weekly mileage. Running 2,500 miles in a year means a little under 50 miles a week. If you miss ten miles one week, that's an extra ten the following week to catch up on top of an already high mileage base. If that's too much, pick a number that's an achievable challenge.

If you're feeling ambitious, follow in the well-worn footsteps of Ben Smith who on 1 September 2015 started a streak with the intention of running 401 marathons in 401 days. On 5 October 2016, the remarkable runner achieved his epic goal.

His aim wasn't just to run the equivalent of a marathon every day, but to shine a spotlight on anti-bullying, raise funds for two charities and 'inspire and challenge people to achieve things they never thought possible'. At the end of his last run, Ben said, 'I was badly bullied for eight years of my life and it affected my self-esteem and confidence so much so that the only way I felt I could get out of that was to try to take my own life when I was 18. The money we're trying to raise is going to support these charities to make sure that what happened to me doesn't happen to anyone else.' Along the way, Ben ran up some eye-opening numbers helped along by many thousands of people who supported him by running, donating and listening to what he had to say.

BEN'S ACHIEVEMENT IN NUMBERS

- Number of miles run – **10,506.2**
- Number of people who ran with Ben – **9,873**
- Number of pairs of trainers worn – **23**
- Calories burned – **2.9 million**
- Amount donated (as of January 2017) – **£315,481.56**

THE END'S IN SIGHT

Every streaker will have their own goals and reasons for running every day. A streak doesn't have to be measured in years or in distances covered by the likes of Ben Smith. A streaker doesn't have to dodge rattlesnakes or run through deserts like Kathy Chase, nor do they have to hobble out of a hospital ward like Ron Hill. A runner can lace up their shoes and start a streak whenever they want. A streak isn't just about collating numbers. It's also about enjoying the love of running, which will mean different things to each runner. It is about inspiring yourself and others around you. When you're out in the cold, rain, wind or snow, experiencing the worst weather conditions that nature has to offer and yet you pity the poor drivers zipping past in their warm cars, radios on, with unfrozen fingertips, you will have become a runner. Do that seven days in a row and you will have become a streaker. Do that for 2,340 weeks in a row and you will become a Covert. Now that is a challenge.

ONE FOR THE ROAD

❝ *When you're in jail, a good friend will be trying to bail you out. A best friend will be in the cell next to you saying, 'Damn, that was fun.'* **❞**

GROUCHO MARX

IN VINO VERITAS

Marathon running and partaking of a tipple have been linked since the inaugural Olympic race in Athens on 10 April 1886. Eighteen runners lined up on the start line that day, with only four of the number being non-Greek, all of whom were allowed to use their own drinks (regardless of what was in them). The use of alcohol and poison as a performance-enhancing substance was already by then a well-established practice in multi-day endurance events, and, as drug testing wasn't introduced until decades later, it is a reasonable assumption that a few of the competitors would have downed a cocktail that would now be banned, as Thomas J. Hicks did eight years later.

Hicks of Cambridge, Massachusetts, won the 1904 St Louis Olympic marathon in a time of 3:28:53, during which he consumed doses of strychnine sulphate (common rat poison at the time and now banned by the International Olympic Committee) mixed with brandy and a raw egg. Due to the choice of race hydration, his coaches had to help him across the line, although he was not disqualified as Dorando Pietri was four years later.

While modern runners tend to steer away from rat poison as their go-to drink of choice, the running world is not, for some, an abstentious one. The late Andy Holden was a remarkable athlete who represented Great Britain in five distance running events on road, fells, cross country, outdoor and indoor track. The *Daily Telegraph* recorded in his obituary, in January 2014, that Holden reputedly drank ten pints of beer the night before winning the Bermuda Marathon in 1979, the same race that saw him beat both Ron Hill's course record and Charlie Spedding, who later won bronze at the Los Angeles Olympics. Holden ran 2:18:50 which is a remarkable time even without a hangover. He won the race in 1980 in a time of 2:15:20 and in 1981 in a time of 2:16:57. The 1979 race is still the one he is most remembered for by many, and his well-known love of the amber nectar stayed with him throughout his career.

Even the modern greats of marathon running dip into the vino from time to time. Portuguese António Coelho Pinto, a 2:06:36 marathoner and the winner of numerous high-profile races, including London on three separate occasions, was so fond of the grape that he once confessed to drinking, on average, four bottles of wine a week and even partaking the night before a race, albeit in moderation.

Many athletic coaches well into the twentieth century believed that alcohol was a performance-enhancing substance. Attitudes have changed with advances in science, but there remains a considerable body of academic research that supports the view that moderate drinking will not harm performance and, in some cases, may even be beneficial. That tends to be with the caveat that it remains within Government guidelines. In excess of that amount, particularly the night before a run or race, and the next day's athletic performance is more likely than not to be below par. Waking up the morning after dehydrated and in need of fatty food is a good predictor that a personal best is unlikely to follow.

THE PROS AND CONS

There are no secrets: distance runners need to be dedicated and disciplined, train hard, lead a simple way of life and not let adversity get in their way.

TONY MILOVSOROV, *RUNNER'S WORLD* READER

Excessive alcohol use and mile-munching don't easily mix. Alcohol is a diuretic and causes dehydration, which in turn causes blood plasma (the liquid covering blood cells in the body) to shrink as the body pulls water from every available source, and this results in numerous pit stops during races. The heart has to work harder to supply blood to the muscles, which causes fatigue, and dehydration means that the body's heat regulator – sweating – will also be adversely affected – so you can't 'sweat out' a hangover during a race. Running whilst hungover also puts a runner at greater risk of muscle strain, electrolyte imbalance and cramps, as the benefits of quinine in that fourth gin and tonic don't balance out the negatives of the alcohol.

Alcohol can have a wide-ranging effect on the brain from difficulty with walking and blurred speech or vision, through to memory loss, blackouts and worse. Combine all of that with a faster or longer run than normal and there is only likely to be one outcome – a tough run. If you can remember it.

Overuse of alcohol can affect the quality and length of sleep, with 3 a.m. trips to the toilet or urgent drinks of water to combat the inevitable dry throat. It can also affect food choice as the ability to make rational decisions decreases with every excessive sip. A healthy option might not seem as appealing as a spicy, calorie-packed late-night takeaway after one too many. The chance of runner's trots and an unsettled stomach appearing the next day are likely to be greater following a vindaloo than the traditional pasta meal. Even the greats are affected by the need for a number two on the run. Look at Paula Radcliffe's famous unscheduled pull-over in the 2005 London Marathon, which didn't prevent her from going on to win in a time of 2:17:42 in what was the third-fastest women's time ever. While Paula's stop was unlikely to have been caused by a poor diet she was none-the-less a relieved woman in every sense.

So, does a life of teetotalism beckon the runner? Well, no. Studies have shown that exercise produces numerous health benefits for the brain and body. The more we run, the greater the prospect that we will have a positive association with moderate alcohol use, according to *Frontiers in Psychiatry*. A runner who drops a few pounds or gains a few seconds in a race is more likely to give the extra one for the road a miss in the pursuit of increased athletic performance and an extra mile on the road. *The Archives of Dermatology* reported in May 2012 that the risk of psoriasis can be reduced by up to 25 per cent by running more than 105 minutes per week. In 2009, the University of Miami published a study on the relationship between alcohol consumption and physical activity. It found that, when compared with current alcohol abstainers, light, moderate and heavy drinkers exercised 5.7, 10.1 and 19.9 more minutes per week. The heavier the drinker, the greater chance they would exercise vigorously during the week. It seems that running and alcohol can be combined. A problem only tends to arise when the latter takes precedence over the former. That is why renowned beer-glugger Bill Werbeniuk played snooker and teetotaller Mo Farah runs. In Werbeniuk's case, he would drink on average six pints of lager *before* a match, which he famously sought to offset as a tax-deductible expense, and then on average one pint for each frame *during* the match. It doesn't require a medical degree to work out what that sort of consumption would do to a runner, who would have trouble in even getting to the start line.

Moderate alcohol consumption may have some surprising health benefits for some runners. Red wine might help stimulate the production of a healthy heart chemical called resveratrol, which inhibits the development of fat cells around the waist and aids respiration. Research has shown that beer can reduce the risk of heart disease by up to 25 per cent, lower the risk of developing kidney stones, experiencing a stroke, developing cataracts or diabetes and can promote bone density. Even taking just a sip of a cold beer could help the body naturally stimulate the production of dopamine, which is commonly prescribed by GPs to help those suffering from insomnia. In short, a little bit of something every now and then at the right time is unlikely to hinder a runner's training schedule or race.

By and large, runners train hard and can party at the same level as everyone else – at least when not training for specific events. It takes a good deal of commitment, desire and hard work to train for races and every so often a night on the town can benefit a training regime. It gives a runner something to focus on as a reward for getting up at 5.30 a.m. for that essential 6-mile run, or forcing tired limbs out the door into howling wind, pouring rain or temperatures so cold that fingertips become numb. For many, the race itself is the reward and the training is part of the experience. But a 12- or 16-week training schedule is a long time and the odd night off here and there might even help a runner to stay on track, with short-term goals eventually leading to the main event.

THE RACES

The organisers of the Berlin Marathon give runners a glass of *alkoholfrei* beer at the finish, which doesn't taste nearly as nice as the real thing (which is likely to be consumed with a bratwurst not long after). The Médoc Marathon in France provides runners and boozers with the opportunity to combine both cultures. Limited to 8,500 entrants, 90 per cent of whom will be in fancy dress, the race began in 1984 and should be on every runner's to-do list. It has 52 entertainment events along the route and 22 refreshment stops serving wine, oysters, ham, cheese and ice cream. Finishers receive a bottle of wine in the bulging goody bag. Personal-best hunters are discouraged, serious athletes frowned upon and personal-worst times are the norm. With all that food and wine, the challenge is to finish, let alone worry about time, which, chances are, will be forgotten by the next day anyway. Adding the odd alcoholic beverage to a training plan in moderation is fine, but abstinence the week before a race is recommended even for those attempting the Médoc.

The race has led to copycat events all over the world including the Bacchus Marathon in the UK. The route goes through the picturesque Denbies wine estate, which encourages runners to take part in fancy dress over quite a demanding course where wine tasting is on offer at each refreshment stop. It may feel a little bizarre at the start lining up next to Darth Vader, semi-naked centurions or Cinderella but by the third or fourth vino stop, it all makes perfect sense. At the end of the race, the answer to the question, 'Where's Wally?', will be perfectly obvious as your double vision will lead to him popping up everywhere.

The Great British Beerathon is a five-mile fancy dress road run in London with 'slobstacles' replacing traditional obstacles. The slobstacles are tables full of food and drink requiring non-nutritious items to be consumed at the end of each mile. The first delightful combination is a pint of bitter and a Scotch egg, followed in subsequent miles by lager and Cornish pasty, cider and pork pie, all washed down with a belly-busting Guinness and crumble. The thoughtful organisers also offer vegetarian options. The first world record of 00:56:45 for the event was recorded in its first outing in 2010, although only 11 results were recorded as 'the marshals became too drunk to care'. By 2016, the record was claimed by Mark Delahunty who won in 00:29:20, which is seriously quick given the nature of the event. With other events called Beat the Barrel – a relay event carrying and then drinking a 36-pint barrel of beer, naturally – Let's get Shitraced and King of the SpHill, the target demographic clearly has one thing in common: they like running and drinking alcohol to excess. So far, there have been no reported serious medical difficulties following the event and, in 2015, one runner even reported waking up the next day without a hangover. He clearly didn't try hard enough.

If Beat the Barrel isn't tough enough for you, The Great Kinder Beer Barrel Challenge may be more up your isolated trail, as it involves climbing 2,087 ft with a barrel and kit weighing 120 lb. A team of eight runners have to lug the gear up very steep slopes from the Snake Pass Inn, across the peat bogs of Kinder Plateau in the Peak District, and past several aircraft wrecks before asking for a jar of the landlady's finest in the Old Nags Head Inn. Pasties, Scotch eggs and the like are optional. The scenery isn't the only thing to take your breath away in this race.

The Shamrock 5 k Beer Run in Indianapolis, Indiana, tempts runners with a beer every kilometre and medals that double as bottle-openers. Given the 10 a.m. start, an afternoon nap is often required after the run.

FASCINATING FACT

· ·

Andrew Fargus has won the Beerathon three years in a row. In 2013 he clocked 00:38:42, in 2014 he achieved 00:39:02 and in 2015 he ran a time of 00:30:43 when he clearly took training seriously and rigorously munched his way through pork pies and pasties all year long in the lead-up to the event.

THE BEER MILE

The Beer Mile is a phenomenon that has its roots in America and Canada. It soon spread across the pond and continues to grow in countries around the world. One of the first beer miles can be traced back to 1989 when seven young friends and athletes lined up on a track at Burlington Central High School and prized open the first ring pull of thousands that would eventually follow. As much a subculture as a race, the concept of the beer mile is simple: run four fast laps of a 400 m track and drink four pints of beer. The challenge grew in university campuses and a brief search of YouTube confirms that British students adopted the challenge with some gusto. It's now extended beyond student life and can be found in events all around the world including Austin, Texas, Launceston, Australia, Iroquois Falls, Canada, Tokyo, Japan, and even Hitchin, England. As it's not recognised by the IAAF or any athletic governing body, the unofficial rules are not set in tablets of stone. In general, they are as follows:

Each runner must drink a can of beer before the start of each lap.

Beer must be consumed within a 10 m transition area at the race start/finish.

Standard cans not less than 355 ml or 12 oz are used and must be opened in the transition area.

Beer must be at least 5 per cent alcohol by volume, fermented from malted cereal grains and flavoured with hops.

Vomiting during the challenge incurs an extra lap penalty.

Patrick Butler created the first known beer mile database allowing runners to log their times, and it has become the go-to resource. In 2003, beermile.com logged 421 recorded beer miles and by 2016 this had grown to 114,320 entries with 7,230 races. The likelihood is that there are many more beer miles that have not been recorded on the website.

The concept is simple although the execution isn't, unless you are 44-year-old mother of six, Chris Kimbrough, who clocked a staggering 6:28.06 in her first attempt on 2 November 2014, or Budweiser specialist, James 'The Beast' Nielsen, who ran it in 4:57 becoming the first official finisher under five minutes on 27 May 2014. By 2016, the YouTube video of his run had been watched 1,584,552 times.

In July 2016, London hosted the first Beer Mile World Classic following on from the FloTrack Beer Mile World Championships which started in December 2014, when Corey Gallagher and Elizabeth Hendon claimed the men's and women's titles. The times that have been posted since The Beast ran the beer mile equivalent of the 1954 Bannister sub-four-minute mile illustrate the calibre of the athletes who are drawn to the race. The current male best is held by Canadian Corey Bellemore, who ran 4:34.35 in London, and the current female best time of 6:08.51 is held by American Erin O'Mara. The vast majority of participants, however, are not elite runners. At the other end of the scale are the likes of Kaylie 'Worst Beer Runner Ever' Iserhoff who posted 37 minutes 52 seconds in July 2009. By April 2010 Kaylie's sobriquet had transformed to 'three-quart' but her crowning glory was a year earlier when she ran 10:36 under the title 'Thunder BadAss' winning the women's event in the process. It seems that the nickname is as important to some as the beer and running.

BRIEF BEER MILE HISTORY

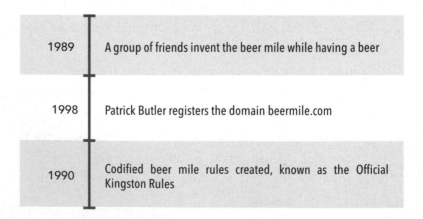

1989	A group of friends invent the beer mile while having a beer
1998	Patrick Butler registers the domain beermile.com
1990	Codified beer mile rules created, known as the Official Kingston Rules

1992	Graham Hood runs a beer mile in 12:11.07, nine weeks after achieving ninth place in 1,500 m at the Barcelona Olympics
1992	Jennifer Robertson becomes first recorded female finisher in 14:50
1997	Seanna Robinson runs a new women's best in 6:42
2007	Canadian marathon runner Jim Finlayson runs a beer mile in 5:09 which topped the charts for the next five years until Australian Josh Harris' time of 5:02
2014	James Nielsen runs a beer mile world record in 4:57.1, becoming the first runner to dip under the 5-minute-mile barrier
2014	Chris Kimbrough nabs the women's record in 6:28.6; in the same year Andrea Fisher lowers the record to 6:28.2 and then Elizabeth Herndon to 6:17.2
2014	FloTrack Beer Mile World Championships begin in Austin, Texas
2015	American Erin O'Mara claims the women's world record in 6:08
2016	Corey Bellemore claims the men's world record in the first international Beer Mile World Classic
2017 and beyond	The owners of Budweiser, far and away the beer choice for may racers, laugh all the way to the bank as profits soar ever upwards

TWO BEERS OR NOT TWO BEERS? THAT IS THE QUESTION

One particularly detrimental effect of alcohol which hasn't yet formed the basis of a clinical study, is the social media announcement. Rash promises to run a race broadcast on Facebook, Twitter or whatever platform is the flavour of the day, made via the empty bottom of a wine glass after a few too many can lead to acute embarrassment in the cold light of day. If you think you want to run a marathon, make that decision while you're stone-cold sober and not while staring through beer goggles into a mirror thinking 'That's a good way of knocking off a few pounds.' It's worth considering the words of Will Rogers: 'We can't all be heroes because someone has to sit on the curb and clap as they go by.' If you want to be a hero, decide before the glass of red and not after.

CONCLUSION

There has never been a better time to be an athlete than right now. Poor old Pheidippides didn't have the advantages that today's runners do, and he paid the penalty. We have at our fingertips easily accessible nutritional advice, training plans and support from a multitude of social-media websites. Advances in specialist clothing, training shoes for every terrain, satellite-navigation watches, hydration packs and pocket-sized gadgets that carry 10,000 songs all make a runner's life a lot easier. All we have to do is head out the door and find a route, race or challenge. There are different running events in Britain, and abroad, every single weekend of the year. We can take part in events involving thousands of people, head for the trails and revel in splendid isolation or join a team of friends as they wade through mudbaths trying not to be electrocuted. Or we can just leave the gadgets behind and simply run, whenever or wherever we want. That's the real joy of running.

'An absolute tonic –
and a very funny read'
Paul Tonkinson
Runner's World

FROM THE CO-AUTHOR
OF THE BESTSELLING
RUNNING MADE EASY

YOUR PACE
OR MINE?

WHAT RUNNING TAUGHT
ME ABOUT LIFE, LAUGHTER
AND COMING LAST

LISA
JACKSON

FOREWORD BY RUNNING LEGEND
KATHRINE SWITZER

YOUR PACE OR MINE?

What Running Taught Me About Life, Laughter and Coming Last

Lisa Jackson

£9.99

Paperback

ISBN: 978-1-84953-827-5

Lisa Jackson is a surprising cheerleader for the joys of running. Formerly a committed fitness-phobe, she became a marathon runner at 31, and ran her first 56-mile ultramarathon aged 41. And unlike many runners, Lisa's not afraid to finish last – in fact, she's done so in 20 of the 90-plus marathons she's completed so far.

But this isn't just Lisa's story, it's also that of the extraordinary people she's met along the way – tutu-clad fun-runners, octogenarians, 250-mile ultrarunners – whose tales of loss and laughter are sure to inspire you just as much as they've inspired her. This book is for anyone who longs to experience the sense of connection and achievement that running has to offer, whether you're a nervous novice or a seasoned marathoner dreaming of doing an ultra. An account of the triumph of tenacity over a lack of talent, *Your Pace or Mine?* is proof that running really isn't about the time you do, but the time you have!

If you're interested in finding out more about our books,
find us on Facebook at **Summersdale Publishers**
and follow us on Twitter at **@Summersdale**.

www.summersdale.com